Look Within Or Do Without

13 Qualities Winners All Share

By

Tom Bay, Ph.D.

Viva Books

New Delhi | Mumbai | Chennai | Kolkata | Bangalore | Hyderabad | Kochi

First Indian Edition 2003
Reprinted 2008

VIVA BOOKS PRIVATE LIMITED

- 4737/23 Ansari Road, Daryaganj, New Delhi 110 002
E-mail: vivadelhi@vivagroupindia.net, Tel. 42242200
- 76, Service Industries, Shirvane, Sector 1, Nerul, Navi Mumbai 400 706
E-mail: vivamumbai@vivagroupindia.net, Tel. 27721273, 27721274
- Jamals Fazal Chambers, 26 Greams Road, Chennai 600 006
E-mail: vivachennai@vivagroupindia.net, Tel. 28290304, 28294241
- B-103, Jindal Towers, 21/1A/3 Darga Road, Kolkata 700 017
E-mail: vivakolkata@vivagroupindia.net, Tel. 22836381, 22816713
- 7, Sovereign Park Apartments, 56-58, K. R. Road, Basavanagudi, Bangalore 560 004
E-mail: vivabangalore@vivagroupindia.net, Tel. 26607409, 26607410
- 101-102 Mughal Marc Apartments, 3-4-637 to 641, Narayanguda, Hyderabad 500 029
E-mail: vivahyderabad@vivagroupindia.net, Tel. 27564481, 27564482
- Beevi Towers, First Floor, SRM Road, Kaloor, Kochi 682 018, Kerala
E-mail: vivakochi@vivagroupindia.net, Tel: 0484-2403055, 2403056

www.vivagroupindia.com

Published by arrangement with

Career Press
3 Tice Road, PO Box 687
Franklin Lakes
N J 07417
USA

ISBN-10: 81-309-1103-5
ISBN-13: 978-81-309-1103-8

Published by Vinod Vasishtha for Viva Books Private Limited, 4737/23, Ansari Road, Daryaganj, New Delhi 110 002.

Printed and bound by Raj Press, R-3, Inderpuri, New Delhi 110 012.

It is with much respect and humility that I dedicate these pages to the men and women of our national Fire Services, people who actually personify the 13 traits of success described in this book.

When the Orange County (Calif.) Fire Authority Leadership Institute chose my first book, *Change Your Attitude: Creating Success One Thought at a Time*, as one of their course readings, I asked to sit in on their first class. After that class, I was hooked and attended the entire one-year course. I was truly blessed by this opportunity to grow, learn, experience, and enjoy.

Most important, my experience with the Fire Service as a whole—and the Orange County Fire Authority in particular—reinforced my belief that looking within improves not only individuals, but also families, businesses, teams, groups, and friendships. That's because all of us function on a higher level when we develop these traits—as Orange County's firefighters and paramedics have. My thanks to them and may God bless them for their work, commitment, and dedication.

Acknowledgments

As always, a very special thanks to my family: David, Margie, Paul, Renée, Cathy, and Brian Wyatt, my grandson, as well as Lauren Taylor, my granddaughter. My constant inspiration and drive come from this wonderful support group.

Thanks to Kevin Brame and Patrick McIntosh for their special friendship as well as their outstanding design and facilitation of the Orange County (Calif.) Fire Authority Leadership Institute course. What a grand experience!

High fives to my classmates and best of friends: Kevin Pedersen, Jorge Camargo, Andy Kovacs, Brian Stephens, Stephanie LaFon, James McAldin, Dave Cisar, Scott Brown, Matt Vadala, Pete Curran, Karen Peters, Jeff Hoey, Gary Wuchner, Ed Fleming, Dan Runnestrand, John Bond, Randall Adamson, Paul Hunter, Glenn Sekins, Roger James, Stacy Lambeth, Dan Drake, Lori Boyle, Paul Guns, and of course, Chief Chip Prather.

Thanks also to Bernard Curtis, my dear friend and brother, who has been a great teacher for me. Bernard's ability to look within is nothing short of outstanding; that's why working with him is a pure joy. I am looking forward to the publication of our book, tentatively titled *Value-Based Leadership*, and years of successful collaboration with Bernard.

Contents

Preface		9
Introduction ______	The 13 Traits	11
Chapter 1 ________	Disciplined	15
Chapter 2 ________	Self-Confident	31
Chapter 3 ________	Persistent	43
Chapter 4 ________	Progressive	55
Chapter 5 ________	Decisive	71
Chapter 6 ________	Focused	83
Chapter 7 ________	Visionary	99
Chapter 8 ________	Lucky	115
Chapter 9 ________	Excels	129

Chapter 10 ________	Enthusiastic	145
Chapter 11 ________	Purposeful	159
Chapter 12 ________	Improver	175
Chapter 13 ________	Spiritual	189
Epilogue		201
Suggested Reading		203
Bibliography		205
Index		215
About the Author		219

Preface

While lunching with Zig Ziglar, I mentioned that I was writing this book and asked if he had any advice to make it more effective. Zig reminded me that the material in my book was not the problem; after all, as motivational speakers, we both talk about success and live the things we talk about. The problem, Zig said, was this: Would my readers be ready to change after they read my book?

We both know that people change only when they are ready to do so. All who listen to our talks or read our books must possess the desire and energy to change their lives. Otherwise, even though they may nod their heads vigorously in agreement, people who have only good intentions continue trudging along in the same deepening ruts. All who have the energy to read this book can find the energy to change their lives by looking within to develop their personal traits of success.

Choose to Change

NBA coach and motivational speaker Rick Pitino believes not only that success is truly a choice for all of us but also that there is a formula for a lifetime of successful behavior. That's exactly the point of this book. My wish for *Look Within Or Do Without* is that you will choose to change because I have convinced you that 13 traits are true life-changers for the people who look within to develop them. Which and how many traits you choose to develop depends on what you learn when you look within; it's up to you.

Surgeon and author Bernie Siegel agrees that no one can make other people choose to change their lives. Change is strictly a do-it-yourself project that comes from within. Siegel should know: He was a skilled surgeon who—like many doctors—maintained an emotional distance from his patients and their families. Then one day the doctor admitted to himself that he really felt like a failure. Dr. Siegel decided to go by his first name, shave his head in solidarity with his patients who had lost their hair to chemotherapy, and get involved in the lives of his patients. Today, he writes books and gives seminars to teach people how to deal with life's difficulties. As those of us who have battled cancer can attest, looking within is key to recovery.

Look at successful people and you see men and women who reinvented themselves by looking within to develop plans for their lives. At some point, each of them thought something like this: This is where I am and that is where I want to be—and *that's where I am going to be,* because I have a plan for getting there. Then they started reinventing their lives by actually using the powers within themselves to develop the necessary traits of success. I hope that the stories I share throughout the book, stories like that of Bernie Siegel, people whose lives illustrate traits of success, will inspire and energize you to change.

The 13 Traits

For the last 35 years or so, I've been blessed with many opportunities to observe people. I've owned retail stores; sold wholesale products on the road; and worked in the finance, savings and loan, and hospitality industries. All of these experiences give me credibility when I talk to groups today. I've learned a lot about the business sector, and even more about people and success.

While I was working different jobs and making career changes, I found I looked up to certain people because of specific traits they possessed. I began to see a pattern—people who I admired had specific characteristics and were consistently successful, such as a boss with a tremendous belief in a Higher Power, a self-proclaimed lucky salesperson, and a persistent collection agent. Through the years, I noticed that similar traits kept reappearing in many successful people I met. I realized that the traits these people exhibited are 13 basic traits common to successful people. The traits are:

1. Disciplined
2. Self-Confident
3. Persistent
4. Progressive
5. Decisive
6. Focused
7. Visionary
8. Lucky
9. Excels
10. Enthusiastic
11. Purposeful
12. Improver
13. Spiritual

While thinking and talking about these 13 traits, I have determined that the first two traits—discipline and self-confidence—are basic to success, but all 13 traits are intertwined. For instance, you cannot develop luck without having enthusiasm. Another example is that a person needs self-discipline to set priorities based on values. Each chapter defines a trait, gives examples of people with that trait, and describes ways you can work on developing one trait at a time. These 13 traits can form the foundation of the rest of your life—your successful life—as soon as you look within and develop them. Which traits you choose to develop depends on how you define success. Remember, as soon as you choose to develop them, you begin taking ownership of your success.

Write in This Book

Each chapter starts out with a story about one trait of success, discusses the trait and people who exemplify it, and ends with a journaling exercise to help you develop that trait.

I have included journaling because it is such an important aid in developing all the traits of success. Harvard Business School studied the financial situations of their graduates, all of whom would be considered successful people. This study found that 10 years after graduating from Harvard:

- 27 percent needed financial assistance.
- 60 percent were living paycheck to paycheck.
- 10 percent were living comfortably.
- 3 percent were completely financially independent.

This study also explored whether the graduates set goals for themselves:

- The 27 percent had absolutely no goal-setting processes in their lives.
- The 60 percent had basic survival goals, such as living paycheck to paycheck.
- The 10 percent had general goals; they thought they knew where they were going to be in the next five years.
- The 3 percent had written out their goals and steps to reach those goals.

Writing something on paper—even something minimal—gets you fired up: Your written goals give you a standard to meet. They make you accountable because when you look at them later, you can see whether you followed through. When goals are just in your brain they dissipate, so be sure to make use of the 13 journaling exercises in this book.

Chapter 1

Disciplined

Bernie came into being in 1974. I was in a lot of emotional pain in those days. I was a pediatric and general surgeon at Yale. I had a wonderful wife and five beautiful children. My life was a success by most standards, but I was unhappy because the job of being a surgeon was very painful. Like most doctors, I had been trained to view medicine as a mechanical profession and to maintain an emotional distance from sick patients and their families. I treated people's diseases and shielded myself from their lives, and I was so miserable and in so much pain behind the wall I'd built that I was considering leaving medicine.

I decided that before I gave up on medicine I would try a different way of doctoring. I would allow myself to care about the patients I was caring for. Once I'd taken that step, I quickly began to see how bizarre it is to view medicine as a profession in which you stand apart from people. Yes, a surgeon deals with cancer, but these cancers are growing in people, and these people are facing great challenges and an enormous range of experiences and emotions. A surgeon is surrounded by people who are sick, discouraged, afraid, embittered, dying—but also courageous, loving, wise, compassionate, and alive.

A doctor is in a position to help people when they need it most—to teach them, when they confront their mortality, that many of the lessons learned will be gifts, not problems. He is also in a position to learn a great deal about being human.

Success

To make important changes that lead to success, we need to be disciplined—just like Bernie Siegel. For Bernie, success is being human. Despite his apparently successful career and family life, something was missing—until he became a doctor who considered the whole patient. For each of us who looks within, success is personal and depends on many factors in our lives. For me, success means equal achievements in all aspects of life: mental, emotional, spiritual, physical, and financial. All of these areas must be in balance for success. When I look within myself, if I am achieving in only two of these categories but not the other three, then my life is not successful. My overall concept of success is based on the need for balance in life. (If you'd like to read more about this, see the final chapter in my book *Change Your Attitude*.)

Look Within Or Do Without

Best-selling author Wayne Dyer has said that we are born looking out when we should be looking within. When people are looking for answers, their desperation sometimes drives them to look in the wrong places. Regardless of input from cultural influences—family, education, training, environment, or spiritual beliefs—each person's answers lie within that person. Think of a fortune cookie: The good news is inside, waiting to be found. All of the answers to your life questions are within you.

The therapy, counseling, training, teaching, and seminar sessions I've gone through all have featured a single constant: Every instructor, therapist, counselor, or spiritual adviser asks participants to take a look at who they are inside. Even such programs as EST, Lifespring, and Psyworld—programs for which people spend thousands of dollars to be trained or to be beaten up emotionally for a week or two—come down to looking within.

But recognizing that you have the answers isn't enough; you must do something with that knowledge. That's why I say that if you don't look within, you'll do without. We have these answers inside of us because they relate to everything that we control. Similarly, the values in each person's life come from within that person, not from the outside; true goals come from within. They govern who we are and what we want to become. The three attributes required to reach our goals all come from within. They are taking responsibility, being accountable for our decisions and actions, and being able to adapt to reach our goals.

Here Today, Changed Tomorrow

Nothing lasts forever, and even our own private definitions of success evolve as we grow older. The common thread is that for each of us, personal success allows us to spend our lives as we want. Like Bernie Siegel, our definition of success changes as we face different challenges, demands on our time and income, and lifecycle stages.

Fortunately, once you develop the trait of discipline and reevaluate your definition of success, change will not seem so impossible. For example, in 1999, three world-class professional athletes retired: Wayne Gretzky from hockey, John Elway from football, and Michael Jordan from basketball. The discipline that these athletes have developed in pursuing excellence in their sports undoubtedly was invaluable to them as they made their transitions to life after professional sports.

A second example is the Delany sisters. Almost everyone has read one of their books or attended the play or watched the TV show *Having Our Say: The Delany Sisters' First 100 Years.* Sadie Delany was the first black domestic science teacher in New York City's public schools; she died at 109 in 1999. Her sister, Bessie, was a dentist in New York City; she died in 1995 at 104. Why did they live so long? Sadie credits their personal discipline:

> People ask us how we've lived so long, how we got where we did. Well, the key is leading a disciplined life. If you're young, that means working or studying hard. When you're our age, it means exercising every day whether you feel like it or not. A lot of people cringe when they hear the word "discipline." They think it means having no fun. Well, that ain't true, and we're living proof! We have a good time. Some folks today want to do things the easy way. We have a saying, "They want to get there—without going!" And there isn't any such thing. You've got to pay your dues. You've got to work for it.

> Sometimes folks ask us how we put up with racism and sexism to get our advanced college degrees. How could we stand it? Well, what choice did we have? What choice does anyone have? Life's not easy for anyone, despite how it may look. Sometimes you just have to put up with a lot to get the little bit you need.

The Delany sisters' father tried to help them define success: "Daughters, you are college material. You owe it to your nation, to your race, and to yourself to go. And if you don't, then shame on you." Although he had wonderful ideas, Reverend Delany had little money. Both Bessie and Sadie worked as teachers in the South to earn money to attend Columbia University in New York City. Nine of their siblings also moved to New York to escape racial prejudice. Although life in Harlem wasn't perfect, it was better. The Delanys celebrated many successes: their family's success, their own professional successes at a time when most women did not work outside their homes, the civil rights movement, and their independence in their later years.

The Delany sisters were so disciplined that they made their own decisions and chose their own successes. Bessie was a bit sharp-tongued; she said just what she was thinking. Sadie listened politely to advice and then did just as she liked.

Discipline also means defining success for yourself. If you believe someone else can define personal success for you, think again. Say, for example, that although his father sent him to school to study computer science, something inside Eugene wanted to work outdoors. Today Eugene designs software and seems to have followed a path established by someone else. His life is okay; he can pay his bills and save a little. Why rock the boat? I don't think he should, but I do think he needs to recognize that he—not his father—has chosen to design software. If Eugene feels good about where his life is going, he is living his decision. If he does not feel good about his life, Eugene needs to become disciplined and make some changes.

Now that we have established that success is defined differently by each of us, that it is a choice, and that it changes from time to time, we are ready to look at the first of the two basic traits of success.

Develop Personal Discipline

Being disciplined means you are in charge of your life. Many times it is easy to yield control to a bottle of pills, a bottle or six-pack, tobacco, food, emotional blackmail, social status, traumatic memories, fear of failure—the list is endless. Yet it all boils down to the question: Who is in charge of your life? If you cannot answer with a resounding "I am!", discipline is the trait you need to develop.

For example, we hear a lot about the sandwich generation, people with children and parents or older relatives who need care. Those in this generation feel stretched, as though their bosses are in charge of their lives at work, their children at home, and their parents the rest of the time. They feel guilty taking time to relax, exercise, or just hang out. What can they do? Can they regain control before they burn out?

Such people can start by knowing that if they look within, they can find answers to this problem; it only seems like an impossible situation. Realistically, they are bearing all of the responsibility for their extended families. Perhaps it's time to split the burden by redistributing responsibilities.

- Options at work include reducing overtime, working at home sometimes, or taking advantage of flextime or job-sharing. Often, work is not the problem; when it is, it may be time to look for a new job.
- Reduce responsibility at home by distributing some of the work. Kids who have age-appropriate jobs around the house may grouse, but work is good for their self-images. No teen should move away from home without knowing how to wash, iron, cook, and clean. Start them out early; they'll bless you later (it'll take about 20 years, but they will).
- Investigate activities for aged relatives so they are not confined to their homes all the time. Send your kids over to talk to them and do chores for them. Check with social agencies, churches, and civic organizations that sponsor programs for seniors who need help with meals, hygiene, and bill paying.

Will this be easy? No. Will kids complain? Yes. Will aged relatives use emotional blackmail? Possibly. Do these things matter? No. People in "impossible" situations need to use discipline to improve the situation for everyone involved. I firmly believe that all the problems we encounter can be solved by looking within. By devising a plan to achieve success by being more disciplined can be a life-changing experience.

Successful sports teams depend on discipline as well as athletic prowess. For example, athletes are coached to be aware of their strengths and weaknesses as well as their teammates' strengths and weaknesses. This means that a forward with a terrific hook shot should get the basketball when he's open inside the key. Or a guard who makes more than half of her three-point shots should get the ball when she's open outside.

In everyday life, we also use our strengths and compensate for our weaknesses. For instance, one of my strengths is public speaking; I've developed that strength by using my business background, constantly collecting material, and keeping my speeches current. One of my weaknesses is trying to do way too much in a short time. And as someone who often lectures that we have only 1,440 minutes a day, I'm happy to say I've learned how to compensate for overbooking myself. I start with the fact that my time and money are basically the same. (If I buy books or CDs for $100, the return on my investment is the time I spend listening or reading. The opportunity cost is everything else that I could have purchased—say, running shoes—with that $100.)

So, instead of just looking at what needs to be done, I look at each activity's return on investment and opportunity cost. For example, when I have a dozen equally important tasks to accomplish in only two hours, I look at the opportunity cost of each one. By doing whatever has the smallest opportunity cost, I am using my time in the best manner. If you also tend to overbook yourself, resolve to get the highest return on your investment of time by letting the opportunity cost guide you in compensating for your weakness.

Devise a Plan of Attack

NBA coach Rick Pitino calls a plan based on discipline a code of conduct, an organized plan of attack:

> Discipline is our plan, our awareness of where we are starting from and what road to take to arrive at our destination.

Without a plan we end up going in different directions, lost in some personal maze, some labyrinth that just takes us around and around, wasting time and energy and distracting us from our goals. Without a plan, we keep covering old territory.

Some people cover the same territory without moving very far at all. Morning after morning these bleary-eyed people sit on the edge of their beds dreading the day before them. They sigh, "Guess I can get through another day." At night they sigh again, this time with relief because they got through another day. All the while, they hope that tomorrow will be better. What magic will cause the following day to be better? Personal discipline would help, but many people who feel this way also feel they are too busy and rushed to develop it. Or worse yet, they are sure they have not an ounce of discipline in their bodies.

Nourish Your Discipline

Despite claims that some people have absolutely no discipline, everyone can be a disciplined person. Each baby comes into this world with all of the traits needed for success; these traits, however, must be nurtured by our caregivers and later by ourselves. If you are not on speaking terms with self-discipline, start today. Imagine discipline as a seed that must be nurtured in a garden. Plant that seed, water it with kindness, pull out the bad-attitude weeds around it, pick off the self-doubt bugs, and shore it up with some I-can-do-this mulch. Use the steps at the end of this chapter to begin being more disciplined.

People who believe that they are not disciplined might as well have a six-foot-high boulder in their pathway. They think there is nothing they can do: can't lift it, can't push it away, can't go around it because it's too wide, can't climb over it because it's too tall. They need to look at what they can do. For instance, a disciplined person would look at that rock and think, "I'm going to chip away at it for the next five days, 10 days, or 20 days—as long as it takes. I'm going to chip at that boulder by taking off one chunk at a time and moving it to the side. Then, I'll chip off another little chunk and move it to the side. And after chipping enough away, what's left of the boulder will collapse and my pathway will be open."

Being Disciplined

People who are disciplined always find a way, a plan of attack. For instance, if they have no time to exercise, they get up five minutes earlier each day for a week. Then they add another five minutes and keep getting up early until it is a habit. Each week they now have 50 minutes of exercise time, just because one day they began getting up five minutes earlier.

And then, there are people like Kathy. Every day while running I see Kathy wearing her headphones while power walking around my neighborhood. I commented to my wife that Kathy certainly was disciplined. It could be rainy, windy, or foggy, yet she was always out there in the morning and evening. One day, I slowed down and walked beside Kathy, so I wouldn't interrupt her routine. I told her how impressed I was with her discipline and mentioned noticing that she had lost weight.

Kathy thanked me and said she discovered about three years ago that she had a weight problem causing her to be pear-shaped. When she asked the doctor how to reduce, he found that she had a thyroid problem. He prescribed a medication but after a couple of days, she called the doctor and said she preferred not taking the medicine and wanted to try some other things. The doctor said that not taking the medicine would not damage her health, but she would continue to have a weight problem and suggested that she exercise. Kathy promised to get back to him a month later.

Kathy knew losing weight would take a lot of discipline because she's not someone who enjoys pumping iron. So she bought a Sony Walkman and started power walking. During the first week, she was feeling better and encouraged by the loss of a couple of pounds. The longer she walked, the more she realized that her discipline was paying off. She says she'll never have the shape that she would like to have, but walking six miles in the morning and four to six miles in the evening helps her feel and look better. "I don't kill myself, but I do discipline myself. It's a major accomplishment because my health is so important to me," she said.

When you have your priorities in order based on what you value, being disciplined helps you do the job.

Olympians and Children

When I think of people with great discipline, I automatically think of Olympic athletes who give their all to achieve their personal best. Peter Vidmar is a good friend, a great motivational speaker, and the only American to score a perfect 10 in Olympic gymnastics on the pummel horse. He told me it's not the big things that get you the gold; it's staying with it. While a student at UCLA, Peter started working five minutes longer in the gym each day; then he noticed that other athletes started to stay five minutes longer. So he upped his time to an additional 10 minutes .

Other disciplined people are students working their way through college or technical school; people who strictly follow special diets for health reasons; those who stop smoking or indulging in other drugs; people who spend within their means; those who obey traffic laws routinely; and, I think, the children with fatal illnesses who keep trying until their last breaths.

I see this consistently because of my involvement with the Orange County (Calif.) Make-a-Wish Foundation that serves children up to 17 years of age who have life-threatening diseases. Wish-granters and others in this organization also must have tremendous discipline. Once a child requests something, wish-granters must immediately begin making that request come true, because they never know how long the child will live.

Hiram Fong

Whenever someone is the first to do something important, you can be sure that this person is disciplined. Hiram Fong, now in his 90s, is one of those special people. The seventh of 11 children, Fong was earning money before he started school; always willing to work, he sold newspapers, caught fish and crabs, and picked beans.

His parents had left China as indentured servants; they worked in the fields of a sugar plantation in Hawaii. They never learned to read, but encouraged their children to do well in school. After being accepted by the University of Hawaii, Fong had to work for three years to save money for tuition. Just three years later, he completed his studies and graduated with high honors; then Fong immediately began saving for law school.

Rumor has it that when Fong returned to Honolulu with his law degree from Harvard in 1935, he had only a dime in his pocket. Eventually, he founded Honolulu's first multiracial law firm with Chinese, Japanese, Korean, and American partners. This law practice prospered, as did his investments, so much so that Fong was a millionaire when he entered politics. In 1938 he was elected to the legislature of the Territory of Hawaii, where he served as vice-speaker and speaker. After working for Hawaiian statehood, in 1959 Fong became Hawaii's senator in the U.S. Congress where he supported changes in immigration laws.

Hiram Fong was the first Asian-American member of the U.S. Senate. After serving for 13 years, he returned to Hawaii where he started several financial businesses and opened a 725-acre garden to showcase Hawaii's beauty. Note how Fong's discipline helped him throughout his life; whether he was saving money for tuition, attending college, starting a business, or running for the legislature or Senate, discipline helped him to attain his desires.

If you are amazed by Hiram Fong's rags-to-riches story and think he was just lucky, you're right (see Chapter 8). In his early life, his enthusiasm for learning made him quite lucky. Later he was lucky in his business investments; but it was more than luck, it was discipline throughout his life that enabled Fong to achieve success.

Journal Notes About Being Disciplined: Developing the Qualities of Success

Because writing strengthens your resolve, I urge you to use the following spaces to jot down what you plan to do to become more disciplined. You will have a chance to write down what you are doing in each chapter. If you prefer using a computer or separate notebook, that's fine, too. When you finish this book, you'll have a record of how far you've come and a journal full of notes about developing the qualities of success.

To reclaim your life today by becoming more disciplined, take these four steps:

1. Look within to determine how you define success, then write your definition:

2. Make some realistic decisions about what developing the qualities of success means to you; list your decisions in the spaces that follow.
3. Break up those decisions into manageable steps you can take to develop success as you define it. Jot down the steps in the spaces that follow.
4. Take action on the first step. Don't be discouraged if it takes a while to complete that first step. Taking just a baby step forward is better than making no change at all.

Decision 1:

STEP 1:

STEP 2:

STEP 3:

STEP 4:

STEP 5:

RESULT:

Decision 2:

Step 1:

Step 2:

Step 3:

Step 4:

Step 5:

Result:

Decision 3:

STEP 1:

STEP 2:

STEP 3:

STEP 4:

STEP 5:

RESULT:

Decision 4:

Step 1:

Step 2:

Step 3:

Step 4:

Step 5:

Result:

Decision 5:

STEP 1:

STEP 2:

STEP 3:

STEP 4:

STEP 5:

RESULT:

Decision 4:

STEP 1:

STEP 2:

STEP 3:

STEP 4:

STEP 5:

RESULT:

Decision 5:

STEP 1:

STEP 2:

STEP 3:

STEP 4:

STEP 5:

RESULT:

Chapter 2

Self-Confident

Coach Tom Carroll first met Mark when the freshman transferred to Damien High School in LaVerne, Calif. While registering for basketball, Mark mentioned that he played baseball, too. When spring came around, Carroll recognized that this freshman had potential.

By the time Mark graduated, Coach Carroll had decided his pitching—not his hitting—was the best part of his game. "By his senior year he was throwing the ball about 90 miles an hour, had a good curve, and was working on a change-up," Carroll said. Mark earned co-MVP and a baseball scholarship to the University of Southern California.

According to Carroll, "Mark was easy to work with. You never had to worry about his grades, and his work ethic was tremendous." Carroll believes that if coaches teach students to believe in themselves, they can do the unthinkable—even hit 70 home runs in a season as his former student, Mark McGwire, did in 1998.

For a lot of us, one of the bright spots in 1998 was the home run race between Sammy Sosa and Mark McGwire. Both men displayed confidence in themselves, each other, and the game of baseball. They obviously felt good about themselves and capable of handling the pressures of the race with grace. Parents, teachers, and coaches need to be mindful of how their children—not to mention they themselves—can be helped if taught to look within and develop the traits that lead to self-confidence and success. In this chapter, you will meet people with self-confidence and learn how employees' self-confidence affects a company's bottom line.

Nourish Your Self-Confidence

Coach Tom Carroll believes that playing sports helps players have confidence in themselves. When their coaches tell them they can play better, players believe them and perform better; then they begin believing they could do even better. Usually the odds of winning or losing are equal, but believing in themselves always tips the scale toward success. In the real world, too, having enough self-confidence to believe in ourselves tips the scale our way.

As I mentioned in Chapter 1, I am a wish-granter for Make-A-Wish; one of my most important duties is similar to coaching because I reinforce the self-confidence of young people in the Make-A-Wish program during their recovery process. Even though many of these life-threatening illnesses are terminal, building self-confidence is a major part of the program. We do everything we can to help these young people feel good about themselves.

To boost his players' self-confidence, Rick Pitino emphasized players' strengths and downplayed their weaknesses. Whenever Pitino told them what he thought they could do, his players worked hard to achieve that. For instance, Pitino described the transformation of Billy Donovan over one summer from a bench warmer resembling the Pillsbury Doughboy to a different person:

> Lighter; quicker; more confident as a player. When Donovan graduated he was one of the top point guards in the country, leading scorer on the team, and second-round draft choice of the Utah Jazz. Now when he looked into the mirror, someone of value stared back. His self-esteem was sky high. He had learned to minimize his weaknesses and believe in his strengths. He had established a great work ethic, had devised a plan of attack, had begun to see the fruits of his labor, and had seen his self-esteem mushroom.

Developing Traits That Create Self-Confidence

In defining self-esteem, psychologist Nathaniel Branden emphasizes the following:

- Confidence in our ability to think and to cope with the challenges of daily life.

- Confidence in our right to be happy; the feeling of being worthy, deserving, entitled to assert our needs and wants; and to enjoy the fruits of our efforts.

Branden makes the point that we cannot improve our own confidence, and thus self-esteem, or anyone else's; rather, we can develop the qualities that—taken together—give us good reasons to be self-confident. The four qualities that he believes are integral to self-esteem are living consciously, responsibly, purposefully, and with integrity. Anyone who develops these qualities by looking within has every reason to feel confident, to be self-confident.

1. People who live **consciously** are mindful of how their actions affect other people. For example, these disciplined people don't drink and drive. (See Chapter 1.)
2. People who live **responsibly** are accountable for their own behavior. For instance, they strive to do their personal best and could never sell shoddy merchandise. (See Chapter 4.)
3. People who live **purposefully** believe in giving 100 percent. For example, they are committed to excellence in whatever they do. (See Chapter 9.)
4. People with **integrity** stand behind their words and actions. For instance, they follow through decisively on their promises. (See Chapter 5.)

We can create a family environment for ourselves and our children that supports these traits, just as coaches can for their players, schools can for students, and employers can for their employees. By looking within and developing these four qualities, we come to believe that we deserve success and we develop enough confidence in ourselves to have real self-confidence.

By now you have probably noticed that the 13 traits in this book are interwoven. Despite your best efforts to separate out only one trait, you will spontaneously develop other traits leading to success. Incidentally, I am not talking about perfectly developed traits because life is a process; we do the best we can at various times with what we're given. As long as we continue to look within and are patient with ourselves and others, self-confidence and success will be ours.

Rick Pitino points out that transforming your life is like a marathon, not a sprint. Being a runner, I have to agree. During a marathon, even when I hit the wall—that point of utter exhaustion when every cell in my body screams to stop—I know that I will recover, so I continue running. An important part of each person's marathon is asking for the strength and spiritual help needed to persist to the finish line. Chapters 3 and 13 have more to say about persistence and spirituality.

Looking Like a Success

Before you continue reading, stop for a minute and think of two people who are self-confident; they cooperate with others, share their enthusiasm, and try to build consensus. And then, think of two who lack self-esteem; they are self-doubting and insecure, think in terms of you-versus-me, and want to win while others lose. As you picture them in your mind's eye, can you detect any differences in the way these four people look and act? (Do not choose any politicians for this exercise; they are atypical.)

Branden suggests that people with healthy self-esteem have a look all their own because they:

- Project in their faces and manner, in the way they talk and move the pleasure they take in being alive.
- Talk of their accomplishments or shortcomings directly and honestly because they recognize and accept these facts about themselves.
- Give and receive compliments, expressions of affection, and appreciation easily.
- Are open to criticism and comfortable acknowledging mistakes because their self-esteem is not tied to perfection.
- Move and speak easily and spontaneously because they are not at war with themselves.
- Illustrate harmony between what they say and do and how they look, sound, and move.
- Are open to and curious about the new ideas, experiences, and possibilities of life.

- Are less likely to be intimidated or overwhelmed by any feelings of anxiety or insecurity because they have accepted, managed, and risen above them; they rarely find their feelings are impossibly difficult.
- Enjoy the humorous aspects of life in themselves and others.
- Respond flexibly to situations and challenges; are moved by a spirit of inventiveness and even playfulness because they trust their minds and do not see life as a place of doom or defeat.
- Accept assertive, but not belligerent, behavior in themselves and others.
- Preserve a quality of harmony and dignity under conditions of stress.

Rosa Parks

One lady who leaps to mind when I think about people with self-confidence is civil rights activist Rosa Parks. This black seamstress refused to give up her seat to a white man to stand in the back of a segregated bus in Birmingham, Ala. Her action on December 1, 1955, lead to a bus boycott that sparked the national civil rights movement and culminated in the passage of the Civil Rights Act in 1964 and the Voting Rights Act in 1965. Like others who had refused to move to the back of the bus, Parks paid a personal price for her defiance. She was taken from the bus, arrested, and placed in jail. She lost her job and her family was harassed and threatened, causing them to move to Detroit. Despite being in her late 80s, Mrs. Parks is still actively working for civil rights and teaching youngsters civil rights history.

Flo-Jo

Another lady with self-esteem was Florence Griffith-Joyner, an Olympic sprinter with an upbeat personality, outrageous bodysuits, and elaborate nails. This diva of the dash was a Watts gal who never forgot her roots; who overcame a speech impediment, poverty, and weight problems; who never tired of encouraging kids to push themselves to achieve excellence. While training to become an explosive sprinter, she worked as a bank clerk and hairdresser. A UCLA graduate, this track and field legend won four medals in the 1988 Olympics and then retired from competition. Her times for the women's 100- and 200-meter races still have not been surpassed.

During her career Flo-Jo was dogged by rumors of steroid use. "How else could she run so fast?" doubters asked. When she died suddenly at age 38 in the fall of 1998, rumors circulated that she died of a drug overdose. An autopsy found she died of suffocation after an epileptic seizure. Flo-Jo brought style and substance to women's track and field and to our world.

James Lowery

Recently I read about James Lowery, someone who has enough self-confidence to go public about something that few men care to discuss or even think about—breast cancer. Each year only about 1,300 men in the nation get breast cancer; however, it kills 400 men a year because the guys wait too long to see a doctor.

Seventy-four-year-old James Lowery wanted to raise awareness and support for male breast cancer patients. He offered this advice: "Men ought to do like women and check themselves." His doctor added that if they feel "a lump in the breast or any change in the nipple or anything that doesn't look right, they should see a doctor immediately." Lowery should know; when he went to the doctor about a growth on his shoulder, the doctor found the lump in his left breast. After a mastectomy and three months of chemotherapy, Lowery is in remission and takes tamoxifen to prevent a recurrence. James Lowery will never know how many men's lives he has saved by publicizing his own breast cancer.

John Stossel

You've probably seen John Stossel doing a "Give Me a Break" segment on *20/20* or an hour-long report on ABC. This slim, curly-haired, incisive and articulate interviewer certainly doesn't appear to have any self-esteem problems. If you didn't see his 20/20 special on stuttering, you'll be surprised to learn Stossel has overcome a major speech impediment. During that show, he did stutter just a little; this is quite a switch from his usual approach as a persistent—at times very persistent—interviewer. Studies have shown that major speech impediments are tied to poor self-esteem;

Stossel mentioned how difficult it was for him to endure taunts and teasing in school. Through hard work Stossel overcame his speech impediment and, at the same time, developed self-confidence.

Gender Stereotypes

My last example of people who have self-confidence is a whole group of men who are living consciously, responsibly, and purposefully; they have tons of integrity. They are just as brave as those men who first explored North America; these men are changing our gender stereotypes.

I'm talking about the growing number of Mr. Moms—men who take care of their children while their wives earn a living. These men are called on to defend their masculinity often. They feel out of place at support meetings geared to women caring for young children. Cynical folks around them predict that their children will not turn out very well; after all, it is common knowledge that men know absolutely nothing about raising and caring for children! I don't think so.

I think these guys have taken over one of the most difficult jobs around. Divorced fathers and widowers who take care of their children face fewer unkind cracks than men whose wives support the family. Think of the magnitude of choosing to stay home with the kids: This decision affects a person's whole life, especially a career—taking 10 years or more off to raise two kids is not an upwardly mobile way to advance anyone's career. It also affects his family life—relatives love to make cracks. Everyone knows mothers sacrifice and stay home, not fathers. Socially, a few fathers have noticed that some of their friends have become distant. And on and on it goes. People who have enough self-confidence to lead the way always attract criticism from those in the back who lack it.

Companies That Develop Employees Self-Confidence

Self-confidence is even more important in business. Wal-Mart founder Sam Walton often said his most important task as a leader was to develop self-esteem in his people. He knew that to survive and thrive, a business must help its employees grow, because employees treat customers the way they are treated. Amazingly, many businesses are more interested in filling jobs than creating an environment where their employees can develop self-confidence. In successful companies, employees believe that their contributions make a difference. People who don't believe they make a difference have little self-confidence. Often they are unorganized, undisciplined, and discontent; they envy others, are sensitive to criticism, and rarely finish their work.

A sharp businessman, Sam Walton realized that the more troubled a person or organization is, the more defensive their behavior is. The more defensive employees are, the faster customers go elsewhere. In this global economy, any business that does not create an atmosphere where its employees can develop their self-confidence is slowly committing suicide.

Claiming Customer Service

Today survey after survey measures customer service, which is synonymous with the self-confidence of employees. Undoubtedly businesses know that customers value service because they advertise their wonderful customer service; however, many deliver only lip service. Unfortunately, this means their employees' self-confidence isn't being developed and their performance shows it. As a trainer, one point I make over and over again is that if you are going to advertise customer service, you better deliver it.

Years ago I worked for a major store that went to the trouble of calculating exactly how many dollars it took per square foot per selling hour to efficiently staff each area of their selling floor with salespeople. For example, these calculations showed that during a four-hour shift it took 2.5 people to produce the total sales they wanted per square foot for one particular area of the store. Despite these calculations, when store managers had to decide between providing good customer service and making more money, they chose to save money by removing one-half person in that area. They assumed that the two remaining salespeople could hustle a little more and that customers would wait a bit longer.

Another example: Have you tried to phone a bank, store, or company lately? Now that we have toll expressways in California, ads invite drivers to call if they have a problem. Once drivers call this state agency, the system promptly puts them on hold and then plays a message telling them the agency really cares about them. It goes something like, "Your call is important to us. Please stay on the line." Then, they play advertising messages. Ninety seconds later, they repeat how much they really care, and then the advertising messages again. This cycle can continue for up to 15 minutes. Logic tells me that if my call were really important, more employees would be working the phone lines.

At the beginning of many calls to customer service departments, a computer announces the length of time callers will have to wait to speak to a person, or sometimes a computer. Although recorded messages tell us they answer calls in the order they come in, this is not in the least reassuring. Companies blatantly permit extremely long waits so callers become discouraged and hang up, thus clearing the lines for more persistent people. With few exceptions, customer service is a joke in today's business sector.

Nordstrom is one of those exceptions. Nordstrom does an excellent job of developing self-confidence in its employees, and thus has excellent customer service. In each department of the store, associates are free to accompany customers to other departments to save them time. Each associate is instructed to do what it takes to keep customers happy; sometimes this means delivering the merchandise or sending customers to a competitor's store for specific items; at other times it means refunding something the customer thinks came from Nordstrom but was sold by a competitor. Nordstrom treats its associates as managers, whose only job is to take excellent care of their customers.

Journal Notes About Becoming Self-Confident: Developing the Qualities of Success

It's a fact: Self-confident people look like they have self-confidence. Therefore, you need to *act as if* you have self-confidence while you are developing the qualities of living consciously, responsibly, purposefully, and with integrity. Meanwhile, you also can look within for the quiet, comfortable core of yourself—the real you.

By following these four steps, you can act as if you are self-confident while you are developing the qualities that comprise it:

1. Act as if by practicing relaxation because it indicates to others that you are open and satisfied with who you are. Chronically tense people are like billboards with large cracks down their centers; these internal splits are due to self-doubt, self-avoidance, or self-repudiation. Whenever you feel tense, take a deep breath while counting to five; hold it, and then exhale while counting to five. Repeat this breathing exercise five times or until you feel relaxed.
2. Act as if by maintaining a posture that is relaxed, erect, and well-balanced.
   - Relax your face so that your color is good and your skin is vibrant.
   - Relax your jaw; hold your chin naturally and aligned with your body.
   - Relax your shoulders while keeping them erect and pulling your rib cage out of your waist. Relax your neck muscles.
   - Relax your hands so they are graceful and quiet.
   - Relax your arms in a natural way.
3. Act as if by developing a purposeful walk without being aggressive or overbearing.
4. Act as if by developing a modulated voice and clear pronunciation; use an intensity appropriate to the situation.

Jot down how you are doing with these four steps to acting as if. For more information about acting as if, see *Change Your Attitude*.

Step 1: Relaxing

Step 2: Posture

Step 3: Walk

Step 4: Voice

In addition to acting as if, you'll want to begin developing the four qualities of self-confidence: Write down which of your actions worked and which did not:

WHILE I AM DEVELOPING THE QUALITY OF LIVING CONSCIOUSLY:

WHILE I AM DEVELOPING THE QUALITY OF LIVING RESPONSIBLY:

WHILE I AM DEVELOPING THE QUALITY OF LIVING PURPOSEFULLY:

WHILE I AM DEVELOPING THE QUALITY OF INTEGRITY:

Chapter 3

Persistent

> Christy Crandall was disappointed because she hadn't topped her best time of 97 minutes for Newport Beach's 5K Spirit Run. But that didn't stop her from finishing the race. Crandall approached the finish line more than 180 minutes behind the fastest woman who clocked in at 17:35 minutes. With a crutch strapped to each arm, Crandall dragged her legs the last 100 yards to cross the finish line hours after the other runners.
>
> Crandall has cerebral palsy and hoped to do better in the Spirit Run. As she explained, "I trained really hard for this one, but I got slowed down because everyone talked to me. They have good intentions but imagine getting a call on your cell phone in the middle of a marathon." Although Crandall appreciated the good intentions, she pointed out that a one-mile conversation is distracting. Crandall plans to race next year, but not to chat.

What makes a runner with cerebral palsy finish a race she clearly cannot win? Persistence! Christy Crandall's persistence in races mirrors her life.

Persist Unceasingly

In Chapter 1 I discussed developing a plan of action by looking within to decide which changes you want to make in your life to ensure success. To implement that plan you'll need to be persistent. Think of persistence as paying your dues. Each day you work to bring yourself closer to your immediate goal and the more distant goal: success. Persistence changes your *wish* list based on "Wouldn't it be wonderful if...," into a *work* list based on one question: How do I get where I want to be?

Persistence is the continued, steadfast pursuit of an objective despite some form of opposition or impediment. Persistent persons are adept at problem-solving and at working on their own. By now you can see how persistence fits right in with solving problems while you are looking within and working on your own plan of action.

No Persistent Pests Please

Persistence sometimes gets a bad rap; it's the only one of the 13 traits for success that can be overdone with serious consequences. For instance, telephone solicitors and mosquitoes are very persistent pests. You think you are rid of them and they just come right back from another angle. Remember that strategy: When something doesn't work the way you want it to, persist and come at it from another angle. The secret to being persistent is not to be intrusive; know when to call it quits and don't be a bloodsucker.

Effective salespeople are routinely persistent because that is part of their job. They just automatically view every negative argument as an invitation to continue the dialogue. Some salespeople cross the line, however, and become pests. As one sales manager acknowledged, "The pest doesn't take no for an answer, but tries to [force] a sale through with browbeating, nagging, or repetition, [or] insulting persuasion. That's self-defeating and gives our business a real setback. The pest carries a good, tenacious approach to an offensive extreme."

He went on to give an example of someone persisting to the point of being a pest:

> One of our good customers called me last year about one of our new young salesmen.... The customer said, "Hal, I don't like to fink on one of your men, but I thought you'd like to know [so you] could straighten him out right away! Your guy called on me...when I was putting together a presentation for a meeting....I tried to tell your man nicely that I was too busy, but he wouldn't stop. He was so excited about your new machine, he kept right on going. I finally got him out...but I was pretty mad about it at the time."
>
> I didn't like to hear that, but at least we got right on it with the salesman. He had let his own zeal blind him to the customer's needs. He doesn't goof up that way any more, believe me!

Persistent People

People who obstinately refuse to give up usually get the job done. For instance, even though speed skater Bonnie Blair was born into a family of speed skaters, she admitted, "At 12 or 13, I was basically a clod on skates. Everyone kept encouraging me to stick with it, so I did. One positive thing about losing is that it shows you how far you have to go and what you need to do to succeed." Blair did not take speed skating seriously until she was 15. Once she got serious, this five-time Olympic gold medalist persisted and began winning.

Protecting the Guilty

In the following story, actual names have been changed to protect the guilty. I like this story because it shows persistence as well as the act of looking within and the whole planning process for change.

Author Daniel Goleman tells of a Wall Street executive we'll call Winston who persisted in improving his empathy—specifically his ability to read people's reactions and see situations from their perspectives. Before this could happen, someone had to tell Winston the truth. On that dark day Winston learned that his subordinates were terrified of working with him, that people even hid bad news from him. The shocked executive went home and told his family, who understood all too well the feelings expressed by his co-workers. With absolutely no prodding, Winston's family admitted that when their opinions on any given subject did not mesh with his, they, too, were frightened of his temper.

Still scratching his head over how he got to this point, Winston put together this plan to develop his empathy:

1. He sought out a coach to observe his behavior and help him change.
2. Winston worked on developing empathy through practice and feedback.
3. Winston took a week's vacation to a foreign country where he did not speak the language. While there, he looked within and decided to monitor his reactions to the unfamiliar and his openness to people who were different from him. This, he discovered, was a humbling experience.

4. When Winston returned home, he asked his coach to shadow him for parts of the day, several times a week, to critique how he treated people with new or different perspectives.
5. Winston consciously used on-the-job interactions to practice actually listening to ideas that differed from his.
6. Winston had himself videotaped in meetings and asked those who worked for and with him to critique his ability to acknowledge and understand the feelings of others.

After several months, his improved empathy was reflected in his overall improvement on the job; Winston's persistence paid off.

Sitting Pretty

One of the first woman journalists, Anne Royall, knew that John Quincy Adams did not like to talk to her; he clearly and consistently avoided her. However, she was determined to interview him. While researching his schedule one day, Royall discovered that every morning Adams swam in the Potomac River. So the following morning she walked to the bank of the river while Adams was swimming and sat on his clothes until he agreed to grant her an interview.

Lubing Up

As we fast-forward to the 1950s, we find Norm Larson—another persistent person; he saw the need for a lubricant that would protect metals from moisture. With two partners, he set up a company to develop this product and began experimenting. Finally, his 40th try was successful, so he named the product Water Displacement, 40th Attempt. This breakthrough came in 1953; initially Larson's product was used to protect missile skins, such as those found on NASA's early Atlas missiles.

After continued experiments, Larson and his partners discovered other more mundane uses for the product that we know today as WD-40. The product wasn't sold to the public until six years after it was discovered, a true test of persistence. Now 80 percent of U.S. homes contain a can of WD-40.

Lobbying

During his 24 years in the U.S. Senate, John Glenn was persistent about returning to space. He repeatedly lobbied NASA to allow him to carry out experiments on the effects of weightlessness on the elderly. Glenn's lobbying was successful. As a crew member on the *Discovery*, 77-year-old Glenn spent nine days observing the effects of weightlessness on himself. During his first flight 36 years earlier, Glenn orbited the earth three times in the *Friendship 7* capsule; this was the first orbital flight by a U.S. astronaut. With the exception of his brief run for the presidency, John Glenn's entire life illustrates that persistence works.

Good Ideas

Some people can't help themselves; they persist in repeating a good idea. After his flight on the *Discovery* in November of 1998, John Glenn was feted with parades and celebrations in large cities and small towns. As Glenn and his wife, Annie, were waving and beaming, they saw lots of youngsters in the crowd. Whenever he was asked to say a few words, this genuine American hero used the opportunity to talk to the youngsters. He stressed the importance of service to our country and always mentioned how he enjoyed his years of service. Public service and the importance of education have been persistent themes of his for many years. The John Glenn Institute for Public Service and Public Policy at The Ohio State University (OSU) houses Glenn's papers, speeches, and memorabilia. Glenn plans to help formulate institute programs, such as one on antinuclear proliferation, and to teach at OSU and Muskingum College, his alma mater.

Love of the Game

John Elway, the winningest quarterback with 148 wins, persisted for love—of the pigskin, that is. At 39, one of the greatest NFL quarterbacks called it quits in 1999. Elway, who was sacked 516 times, persisted in using the same style of play, knowing that waiting until the last second to pass the football made him a prime target. For me, John Elway's 47 comeback victories make up his most impressive statistic. Not only did he persist with his career in spite of 12 surgeries and injuries to his shoulder, biceps, ankle, rib, and hamstring, but he also persisted in 47 come-from-behind wins. That's persistent leadership.

Refusing to Be Ignored

Some people persist because they don't like to receive a form letter. When she was 9, Melissa Poe was worried about the environment and wrote a letter to then-President George Bush. After receiving a form letter from the president's staff in reply, she convinced a billboard company to donate billboards showcasing her "Dear Mr. President" letter in Washington, D.C. Although she was aiming for the Chief Executive, Poe received a lot of response from kids and started Kids FACE (Kids For A Clean Environment).

After an appearance on the *Today Show*, Poe received even more mail that she personally answered. Meanwhile, her mother wrote to Sam Walton (Wal-Mart founder), who invited Melissa and her mom to an executive board meeting. As a result, Wal-Mart and other corporate sponsors underwrote printing and mailing costs as Kids FACE grew to more than 100,000 members. Meanwhile, Poe's persistence has allowed her to accomplish what she wanted: Kids FACE is helping protect the environment.

Seeing a Need

Some people are persistent because they see a need, as Mary Joan Willard did when she met a 23-year-old quadriplegic named Joe.

> I was shocked. I found it inconceivable that someone so young, so full of life, was going to spend the rest of his days completely dependent on other people...for a drink of water, for a bite of food, for a book, to turn out a light....I kept thinking there has to be a way to make him more independent.

That night Willard kept thinking about the situation and came up with an answer: chimps.

Willard went to see Harvard psychologist B. F. Skinner, for whom she had worked for three years. Skinner pioneered the method of using reward and punishment to alter animals' behavior. After listening thoughtfully to Willard's idea, he pointed out that chimpanzees are almost as big as humans, stronger, and bad-tempered. Skinner suggested using capuchins, which are often called organ-grinder monkeys; they weigh 6 or 7 pounds, are rarely taller than 18 inches, and live about 30 years. They are intelligent, easy to train, and form bonds of loyalty to human masters.

Encouraged by her conversation with Dr. Skinner, Willard read about capuchins, found a supplier, and made an appointment to see the director of postdoctoral programs at Tufts New England Medical Center in Boston, where she had a postdoctoral fellowship. The director nearly fell off his chair laughing at first, but Willard was persistent; later, the director came up with a $2,000 grant and training space.

Those first monkeys learned a variety of tasks: moving food from a refrigerator to a microwave oven; turning on and off lights, a television set, stereo, heater, or an air-conditioner; opening and closing curtains; setting up books, magazines, and computer printouts on a reading stand; picking up a mouthstick and putting it in the quadriplegic's mouth. The capuchins received rewards every time they did tasks correctly.

After the success of the pilot program, the demand for simian aides increased. Willard began spending more time fund-raising and administering the nonprofit program. Of the first 39 grant proposals she sent to foundations, none was approved. In addition to a lack of money, some people thought that using monkeys as helpers was demeaning to the quadriplegics.

Despite its early problems, thanks to Willard's persistence, Helping Hands: Simian Aides for the Disabled has survived and continues to train monkeys for thousands of quadriplegics.

Finding Out If He Had What It Takes

Lonnie Johnson won a state science fair competition with a remote-controlled robot that he built with batteries, compressed air, and tape reels. That was back in 1968, before robots were as common as they are today. While growing up in the South, Johnson was told that he did not have what it took to be an engineer. Even though he was disappointed, Johnson decided to give college a shot anyway. Persistence and brains won out; he received a bachelor's degree in mechanical engineering and a master's degree in nuclear engineering.

At NASA's Jet Propulsion Laboratory, Johnson worked on the *Voyager*, *Mars Observer*, and *Galileo*. In his spare time, this rocket scientist invented and patented various items, the most successful of which was the Super Soaker, a water gun capable of firing a stream of water 50 feet away. More than 250 million soakers have been sold to children and adults. Today Johnson holds 49 patents and persists in developing new ideas at his research company in Smyrna, Ga.

Justice

In June of 1963 Medgar Evers was murdered outside of his Jackson, Miss., home while his wife and three children were inside watching television. Evers had not only opened the NAACP's first office in Mississippi, but he also demanded better jobs, higher pay, and equal schooling for black Americans. He fought the poll taxes and voting tests required of blacks, too.

Myrlie Evers, his wife, promised her husband that his murderers would be punished. It took 30 years, during which time white supremacist Byron De La Beckwith was charged and tried twice. Each time the jury deadlocked and he went free. Evers-Williams recalls:

> People told me I was out of my mind, that no white man was going to jail for murdering a black man in Mississippi, that I should just leave it alone. Friends and relatives were sick of me asking questions, digging into files....But I wouldn't quit.

Evers-Williams persisted even after she moved to California, where she returned to college and supported her children by giving speeches for the NAACP. After graduating and while working, she pursued the man who murdered her husband. Finally, an inquisitive newspaper reporter uncovered evidence of jury tampering and in 1994 De La Beckwith was convicted and sentenced to life in prison.

Civil rights activist Myrlie Evers-Williams comments:

> If you have a goal, pursue it. The quest for justice and equality is not something you do or work on for a couple of years and stop. If you don't guard our freedom, it can be taken away from you.

Journal Notes About Being Persistent: Developing the Qualities of Success

Persistence can help you achieve success both when you look within and later as you develop this trait. Thinking back over your life, choose something that you pursued with persistence. Remember the situation in detail and remember how good you felt about getting what you worked for. What happened as a result of not giving up?

DESCRIBE THE SITUATION AND HOW YOU FELT:

RESULT:

Thinking back over your life, choose something that you pursued briefly before giving up. Remember the situation in detail and remember how you felt about giving up. What happened as a result of your decision to give up?

DESCRIBE THE SITUATION AND HOW YOU FELT:

RESULT:

Choose one of your decisions from Chapter 1 and describe how you can persist in achieving it.

Choose one of your decisions from Chapter 4 and describe how [illegible] in achievement.

Chapter 4

Progressive

During World War II, Kenneth Russell from Louisville, Tenn., parachuted behind German lines on June 5, the day before D-Day. During his descent into Sainte-Mere-Eglise, a small French town, Russell's parachute became entangled on a church gargoyle. Helplessly suspended, he became a prime target for German gunners below.

Fifty-five years later, Russell returned to France to commemorate the anniversary of the D-Day landings. He met one of the German gunners who tried to kill him. Russell said that the gunner "broke down in tears and so I just embraced him. I said I wasn't mad at him. It was a long time ago, so I said I loved him."

Kenneth Russell's story gives us a chance to see two men who have progressed far beyond what they were as young soldiers; it also illustrates how that progress has changed each one. In 1945 each soldier was doing his personal best to win a war. Today, each man is doing his best to heal the ravages of war in himself and others—one by admitting guilt and the other by forgiving; that's real progress.

This war story illustrates an important point—that growth takes place in the lives of those who are progressive. For example, many of the one thousand or so World War II veterans who attended the 1999 commemoration of the D-Day landings are no longer gung-ho about going to war. Even though they are proud of what they did, now they comment, "War is insane. War is the greatest catastrophe known to mankind. It must be avoided at all cost." Brash and brave 20-year-old soldiers have turned into gray-haired veterans still brave enough to speak their minds.

Progressive Living

As a runner, I keep track of my personal best times. If you fish, you probably know to the fraction of an ounce how much the largest fish you ever caught weighed. We all keep track of our progress—for some it may be the length of a golf drive or the amount of food collected for the hungry. For others, it is taking first place in a spelling bee or baking so many dozen donuts. Such examples illustrate that we all understand the concept of making progress; making this success trait part of our lives is more complicated.

Deciding to be progressive means looking within and resolving to go all out to do your best. This has absolutely nothing to do with personal perfection; it just means deciding which things in your life are so important that they deserve your best efforts. Not everything does. Trying to make progress in all areas of your life would be counterproductive because some things in life are not worth your best efforts; for instance, washing your car four times a week. Therefore, before you can work on progressing, you need to look within and to make some choices. As you look within, think of all the areas of your life and decide what part of each area requires you to progress; then, develop a plan of action in the journaling section to act progressively.

Often people choose family and work as areas deserving their best efforts. If you do, remember that even though Fortune 500 CEOs are well paid, they may not necessarily be progressive at work. Salaries rarely reflect the importance of jobs; if they did, teachers and day care workers would be paid a lot more for doing their important jobs. So, don't consider the size of your paycheck as an indicator of whether you are progressing. As Martin Luther King, Jr., said: "If a man is called to be a street sweeper, he should sweep the streets even as Michelangelo painted, or Beethoven composed music, or Shakespeare wrote poetry. He should sweep streets so well that all the hosts of heaven and earth will pause to say, 'here lived a great street sweeper who did his job well.'"

Allow Criticism to Polish Your Mirror

We all love to criticize, although we prefer to say that we are giving advice for someone's own good. Remember that when you are concentrating on being progressive and someone steps up to offer advice about what you could do differently. Bernie Siegel suggests that we listen and evaluate criticism of ourselves; such criticism is an opportunity to become better persons. In the words of the Sufi poet Rumi, "your criticism polishes my mirror." Criticism can help us see ourselves better, and thus progress.

Siegel tells the story of a patient who gave a bottle of liquor to every doctor who had taken care of him during a hospital stay—except Siegel. The patient charged that Siegel was always angry. Siegel explained he was not angry with the patient, but angry about what he had to do to the patient, such as inserting a tube into his windpipe. Then Siegel apologized for his anger. Siegel appreciated the fact that even though the patient was leaving the hospital, "he took the time to criticize because he saw my pain and reached out to help me." As Siegel did, accept criticism as an aid to progressing; evaluate its value and take appropriate criticism to heart.

Being Progressive Can Hurt

When you decide to be progressive, you may come away with bruises, as Hank Aaron did. On April 8, 1974, Hank Aaron hit his 715th home run, breaking Babe Ruth's record. At a celebration afterward, Aaron said to the crowd:

> I would just like to say to all the fans here this evening that I just thank God it's all over with.

What was over was the hostility he faced while chasing the Babe's record. Reflecting on his pursuit of Ruth's record, Aaron recently noted:

> I wish all of it could have been done differently. I would have made it like it was [in 1998] with McGwire and Sosa—you know, a happy moment, going to the ballpark, enjoying yourself, doing what you could do best. I was happy for them; I was happy for baseball....It was the same way when Pete Rose was chasing Ty Cobb's [career hits] record. He seemed to be enjoying it.

Aaron explained just how different his chase was in 1974:

> People were living in the Babe Ruth era; you have to remember that. They were not ready to accept [black players] yet. And here I come along challenging what was one of the most hallowed, most prestigious and biggest records in all of sport.

And people were not about to turn that loose. You still had those die-hard racist people who wanted to hold onto that.

If you think Aaron was exaggerating, remember that in the 1970s, Aaron and other black baseball players stayed in rooming houses on road trips while their white teammates slept in hotels.

While chasing Ruth's record, Aaron received more than 900,000 pieces of mail, many filled with hate, racial epithets, and death threats. In contrast, during McGwire's pursuit of Roger Maris's record he received 100,000 letters, most of which were congratulatory. In 1999 baseball honored Aaron with a 25th season celebration but the sport could not rewrite history so that Aaron's chase would be as pleasant as McGwire and Sosa's.

Ben Hogan's Legacy

Legendary Ben Hogan won 63 PGA Tour events between 1938 and 1959; that places him third behind Sam Snead and Jack Nicklaus. Who knows how many Hogan would have won if he had not served in the U.S. Army Air Corps for two years or had not been forced to battle back from a nearly fatal car crash in 1949.

That lifetime record is the result of Hogan's 12-hour workday; he was on the practice range every night because of his desire to progress. At the opening of the Ben Hogan Room in the USGA Museum in Far Hills, NJ., Valerie Hogan recalled that her husband "always tried to give his very best."

Jack Nicklaus admits trying to emulate Ben Hogan. Nicklaus recalled how Hogan prepared for a tournament on the practice tee: "He was all wrapped up in what he was doing. Other players were talking and making jokes, but not Ben Hogan. I think Hogan invented practice."

Progressing Through Recovery

Sometimes opportunities to do our best are thrust upon us; they defy us to hang tough. Such an opportunity occurred when Army Captain Max Cleland saw a live grenade on the helicopter pad just after he hopped out of a helicopter on a hilltop in Vietnam. Moments later he lost his legs and an arm; days later he blamed his own carelessness, thinking one of his M-26 grenades had done the damage. Returning home, Cleland made a remarkable recovery and continued serving his country at the Veterans Administration and in the U.S. Senate where he represents Georgia.

Cleland was still blaming himself for his lost limbs 31 years later when he received a call from a former Marine. While watching a History Channel program about medics and corpsmen, David Lloyd learned that Cleland thought he had caused his own injuries. So Lloyd called to set Cleland straight; he described a dazed, blood-drenched private who had just arrived in Vietnam. The 18-year-old was crying, "It was my grenade, it was my grenade." After treating the young soldier's wounds, Lloyd discovered the private had straightened the pins on his M-26 grenades to make them easier to activate. To avoid further injuries, Lloyd took them away.

After learning that the private's grenade had caused his injuries, Cleland has gone through an emotional healing; and he still refuses to play the blame game. "If I ever come across that individual," he said, "I would give him a big hug and say, 'Don't worry, don't feel guilty. A thousand things could have happened to us out there.'" What a progressive statement! That progress began when Cleland accepted his wounds and continued through his realization that he still had something to contribute; it culminated in his forgiveness toward someone who changed his life so drastically.

Feeling Responsible to Make Good

Children's author Yoshiko Uchida was a 20-year-old Japanese American student at the University of California in Berkeley when her father was arrested by the Federal Bureau of Investigation in 1941. After her father was sent to a detention camp in Montana, Uchida, her sister, and mother were told to dispose of their possessions. The Uchidas became Family No. 13453 and received tags with this number for their few remaining belongings. Within 10 days, they were sent to San Bruno, Ca., where their home was a 10-by-20-foot horse stall at a racetrack surrounded by a barbed wire fence and guarded by armed soldiers in towers. A week later her father joined his family.

Despite the oppressive conditions, Yoshiko and her sister Kay began teaching school. Four months later the Uchidas were sent to Topaz, Utah, where they continued teaching. The family lived in one room of tar paper barracks on the edge of a desert. Severe snowstorms plagued them in the winter and dust storms in the summer. Uchida wrote:

> The wind reached such force we thought our barrack would be torn from its feeble foundations. Pebbles and rocks rained against the walls....The air was so thick with smoke—like dust, my mouth was gritty with it and my lungs seemed penetrated by it. For hours the wind shrieked around our shuddering barrack.

The next year Kay was offered a job in a nursery school and Yoshiko was allowed to attend graduate school at Smith College. Yoshiko left the detention camp determined to prove that the Americans who discriminated against people of Japanese ancestry were wrong.

> I felt a tremendous sense of responsibility to make good, not just for myself, but for all Japanese Americans....It was sometimes an awesome burden to bear.

After World War II ended, Uchida received a fellowship to study in Japan; these studies deepened her pride in her Japanese heritage. Returning to the United States, Uchida fulfilled her progressive goal to make good for all Japanese Americans by writing books for young people. She wrote more than 28 and a memoir of life in the detention camps for adults. Her themes were often stories of her own past in which pride and perseverance overcame discrimination and imprisonment.

Following Dreams

As I mentioned earlier, being progressive sometimes involves making a change. Long-held dreams and desires to progress are reasons people chuck one career and start all over in a new one. Gradually they look within and realize they can no longer do their personal best in their current positions.

Take for example, David Werner, who once presented closing arguments to a jury; now he entertains audiences with his political humor and songs. His act centers around current events and politics. So, how's he doing? He said he's "pleased with the numbers, but it's the time and independence that's important."

While in school, Werner acted in plays and musicals; at Yale he performed with the "Law Review." Later he told jokes in comedy clubs and performed with the Capitol Steps, a musical satire troupe. When he noticed he had to turn down comedy jobs because he was working as a lawyer, Werner had to make a choice and decided to change jobs. "There is that moment when you are jumping off [into a new career] and you hope the parachute opens," he said. That's all part of putting forth a progressive effort.

Another example is Tina Tang, who worked on Wall Street as a financial analyst. What would make her abandon a six-figure salary? She says, "Everyone I worked with was smart, but I wanted to do something that I felt I could be the best at. People were making really good money but didn't seem particularly thrilled with their work. I didn't want to feel trapped because of the money."

Two years ago she began making and selling jewelry full time; previously this had been her hobby. Tang makes all of her jewelry by hand. She hopes to increase her sales so she can concentrate on design and marketing while a manufacturer produces her line of jewelry. She commented, "owning your own business is the ultimate professional endeavor."

Changing the Social Order

Myra Colby Bradwell, Esq. is not a well-known historical figure, but what a woman she was! Her progressive efforts included being the first female lawyer, an advocate for women and children, a community leader, and a successful businessperson.

After the Civil War, when Myra told her lawyer husband that she wanted to read law and take the Illinois state bar exam, James offered to help her. Myra passed the exam in a way deemed "most creditable" but her application to become a lawyer was denied because she had a disability—she was married. Legally, she did not exist independently from her husband. Myra Bradwell fired back a brief that forced the court to say what they meant the first time: she could not practice law in Illinois because she was a woman. Her reply was to petition the U.S. Supreme Court; several years later the Court upheld Illinois's right to refuse her application to be a lawyer. Twenty-one years after her request, the Illinois Supreme Court passed a retroactive decision admitting Bradwell to the state bar in 1890.

In 1868, Bradwell recognized the need for a weekly legal newspaper and started the Chicago Legal News, which was a digest of legal information; general news; and recently passed laws in Illinois, other states, and the nation. Always an astute businesswoman,

Bradwell also established a legal publishing, printing, and binding company. She received a special charter from Illinois allowing her to be president of both companies; as a woman she lacked the legal status to own a company. Both of her companies were successful enough to make her wealthy. More important, these firms gave her a powerful voice in the legal system; although she could not argue a case in court, the courts allowed her newspaper to be used as evidence. Whether the lawyers and judges liked it or not, Myra Bradwell was practicing law through her paper.

When the Chicago fire destroyed her newspaper building in 1871, Bradwell boarded a train to Milwaukee, where she wrote the paper and had it printed. Later she worked hard on the committee that planned the rebuilding of Chicago. In addition to proposing numerous reforms for the legal profession, Bradwell talked congressmen into choosing Chicago as the site of the 1893 Columbian Exposition. After her death, her daughter, also a lawyer named Myra, took over the legal newspaper.

Companies Pursue Progressive Goals

Each year *Fortune* magazine publishes a survey of the best places to work in the United States. Being ranked means that these companies are progressively trying to develop their employees. In 1998 I found some interesting attitudes in two of the companies ranked: At Worthington Industries in Worthington, Ohio, chairman and CEO John H. McConnell commented about founder John P. McConnell's philosophy:

> It's always been part of my father's philosophy: Treat people with respect and give them an opportunity to grow— people will give back far more than you ever give them. These are life principles, not business principles.

A firm that progressively gives to its employees receives the best from each employee.

TDIndustries, a Dallas-based plumbing and air-conditioning contractor, was ranked second best by *Fortune*. President Ben Houston believes that "If we are to lead, we must collectively take input from our employees." Houston is concerned with negative input as well as positive. For example, he mentioned that 90 percent of his employees thought that its camaraderie made TDI a great place to work. Sounds good to me, but to Houston, that meant 110 employees do not think they have great camaraderie so there's room to progress.

TDI was founded in 1946 and opened to employee ownership six years later. Today employees own three-quarters of the stock and the top 30 officials own the rest. The company's mission statement is "We are committed to providing outstanding career opportunities by exceeding our customers' expectations through continuous aggressive improvement." Notice that the career opportunities of workers are mentioned before customer service. Standing behind this mission statement are competitive salaries and benefits and 32 hours of employee-chosen training each year. It's good to see that some progressive companies are doing their best to facilitate employees' desire to give their best efforts.

Bringing a Little Something Extra to Work

Progressive workers do their best, which changes the way they look at their jobs and often causes them to willingly do more than is expected. Jimmy Conklin, the delivery man for Sir Speedy in California, has a lifetime of progressive efforts at work. He says "I never had a job in my life that I didn't try to do the best that [that] job has ever been done." After World War II, Conklin took a temporary job at Uniroyal Tire Company; by the time he retired 32 years later, he had worked his way into supervisory jobs.

For the next 15 years he owned and operated a Quick Copy shop. When Conklin sold the shop, he delivered cookies and personalized notepads to potential customers to help his successor get a good start.

In 1993 he started delivering for Sir Speedy, a copy shop in Laguna Hills. Seventy-three-year-old Conklin drives about 125 miles a day delivering quickprint orders and making friends by dropping off something extra—his cookies. He also began making what salespeople call cold calls; he "decided to take cookies and pads to businesses and tell them if they needed any printing to call me. No hard sell." He bakes about 80 to 100 cookies each night and an occasional carrot cake or banana nut bread. After his boss accidentally learned about Conklin's cookie deliveries, Sir Speedy bought Conklin an industrial mixer and began paying for his cookie ingredients.

Journal Notes About Being Progressive: Developing the Qualities of Success

While considering each of the following areas, look within to discern one specific part to focus your best progressive efforts on. Then briefly describe that one part on the line next to each area; next, go back and jot down the steps to take so you have a plan of action for progressing in each area.

After working on the first area of your life for 21 days, write down how things are going, what works, and what does not. Before you begin working on the second area, review what you did in your first area. Then determine how you could use what you learned in pursuing your first goal while progressing toward your second goal. Proceed in the same fashion through each of the five areas.

FAMILY: ______

STEP 1: ______

STEP 2: ______

STEP 3: ______

STEP 4 ______

STEP 5: ______

WHAT WORKED: ______

WHAT DID NOT WORK: ______

WORK:

STEP 1:

STEP 2

STEP 3:

STEP 4:

STEP 5:

WHAT WORKED:

WHAT DID NOT WORK:

COMMUNITY:

STEP 1:

STEP 2:

STEP 3:

STEP 4:

STEP 5:

WHAT WORKED:

WHAT DID NOT WORK:

SOCIAL:

STEP 1:

STEP 2:

STEP 3:

STEP 4:

STEP 5:

WHAT WORKED:

WHAT DID NOT WORK:

SPIRITUAL: __________

STEP 1: __________

STEP 2: __________

STEP 3: __________

STEP 4: __________

STEP 5: __________

WHAT WORKED: __________

WHAT DID NOT WORK: __________

Chapter 5

Decisive

In 1908 William Hoover realized that before long automobiles would destroy his business of making leather accessories for horse-drawn carriages, so he started the Electric Suction Sweeper Company.

In 1924 Robert E. Wood's idea of moving into retailing was rejected by Montgomery Ward. So he went to another catalog company, Sears, Roebuck & Company, which bought the idea and opened its first retail store in 1925. Sears became the world's largest general merchandiser.

In 1950 Frank McNamara forgot his cash one evening when he went out to eat, causing him to develop the first credit card, the Diners Club Card.

In 1952 Kemmons Wilson built the first mid-priced Holiday Inn in Memphis, Tenn., because he and his family were disappointed by the expensive and/or dirty motels they encountered on vacation.

In 1961 Jean Nidetch went to the Obesity Clinic at the NYC Department of Health. She invited six dieting friends to meet once a week at her Queens apartment to compare notes. These were the original Weight Watchers meetings.

In 1979 Ernest Thomke developed the Swatch watch that increased the Swiss watch industry's market share from 15 to more than 50 percent almost overnight.

In 1980 Ted Turner ignored market research and naysayers who predicted that a 24-hour news network would not survive and started the Cable News Network (CNN).

In 1980 Sony began distributing the Walkman because Akito Morita noticed that young people liked listening to music wherever they went. Morita decided that no market research was necessary because "the public does not know what is possible. We do."

Each of these people made one basic decision that required hundreds of other decisions down the road. By being decisive, each created a niche for something new, whether it was a mid-priced motel or a carpet sweeper. Similarly, each of us makes family, business, moral, social, and community decisions that have lasting effects. The decision to place an elderly relative in an assisted-living facility is no less gut-wrenching than deciding how many people to furlough due to a work slowdown. No matter what the decision is, looking within and being decisive makes it easier to find answers to problems or to choose between two objectives. That's why decisiveness is so important to our success and well-being.

Next we'll look at the characteristics of decisive people, the steps in making a decision, and the fears that prevent people from making any decisions.

Decide to Be Decisive

Decisive people are flexible and take the initiative; they are oriented toward action, achievement, and results. For example, when working on a committee, in a family, or with a social group, a decisive person:

- Recognizes that the group needs to identify long-term goals and tries to keep everyone focused on enhancing these goals through their decisions.
- Works to get closure on critical issues by suggesting that an idea has been studied long enough and it's time to make a decision.
- Realizes that the issues to be considered may increase in number and complexity.
- Refuses to adopt an I-told-you-so attitude when someone else's suggestion does not pan out.

Because of their self-awareness, decisive people are able to make decisions that mesh with their values. For instance, if a decisive person went to a garage sale where many brand-new electronics items were on sale, that decisive person may decide not to buy a new TV set there. The price would be right, but the suspicion that the merchandise was stolen would encourage a decisive person to leave empty-handed.

Similarly, if a friend or relative has a drug or alcohol problem, we have two choices: Organizing an intervention to make the friend or relative face facts and get treatment, or accepting things as they are and hoping for the best. The first choice could mean temporary alienation or complete loss of a friendship. The second choice could mean attending a friend or relative's funeral. A decisive person who values friendships would begin organizing; an indecisive person would wait and see.

Steps to Making Decisions

Unlike a 2-year-old who has just learned to say no, most of us have to work on acquiring such decisiveness later in life. If you're the type of person who spends 15 minutes choosing a melon at the market, use the following steps to speed up your decision-making:

1. Determine your objectives. Look within so that you are really clear about what you are aiming for and what you will go through to get it. Do you want something that is perfect or something that is fast?
2. Consider the worst things that can happen as a result of your decision. Can you accept those consequences?
3. Take some time to examine all the angles. Learn to act as quickly as you must; when there is time, weigh your options; when there is no time, decide.
4. When you come to an impasse, ask yourself how someone you admire would handle the decision.
5. Ask for advice from someone who has made similar decisions.
6. Make a list with pros and cons side by side, using only a few key words.

After you have made your decision, don't second-guess yourself. Celebrate your good decisions and analyze the not-so-good decisions by looking within to improve your decisiveness. Remember that you have the answers you need in your life, but they won't do you any good unless you look for them.

Fear Destroys Decisiveness

At some time or other, each of us has worried, "What if I make the wrong decision?" The next time you question your decision-making ability, remember Captain David Glasgow Farragut's instruction during the battle of Mobile Bay in 1864: "Damn the torpedoes—full speed ahead!" Then, use the previously mentioned steps when making decisions, so you'll have a better-than-even chance of making great decisions.

Fear literally freezes our minds and bodies; we can feel our muscles tighten up. Psychologist Virginia Satir commented, "When your body feels tight, your brain often freezes right along with your tight body, and so your thinking becomes limited as well." When you feel yourself freezing up, breathe deeply to relax and look within for reassurance that you can make a good decision. Fears that can torpedo your ability to make up your mind include: failure, your feeling of unworthiness, fear of looking foolish, fear of the unknown, and change. Let's take a brief look at each.

Fear of Failure

Most often, fear of failure does not cause you to make the wrong decision, but to make no decision. Remember that a lot of people fail and live to tell about it. Harry Truman failed as a shopkeeper but succeeded when he picked up the reins of a government embroiled in a world war. Thomas Edison failed thousands of times, but we remember only his successes, such as the light bulb and phonograph. Fear of failure causes us to distrust our ability to think, learn, and make decisions.

Dave Longaberger knew all about failure—he stuttered, was an epileptic, and repeated the 5th grade three times. Later he watched his sizable investment in several grocery stores disappear. Longaberger realized that failure wasn't fatal, however, and started up a new business venture. The result was Longaberger Company, the nation's largest handmade basket-making business, a $700-million business with 54,000 basket weavers and in-home sales associates in 1999.

In the 1980s Longaberger again flirted with bankruptcy, but turned things around. As soon as the company was on firm ground, he decisively started fulfilling his dreams: He added pottery, wrought-iron furniture, and accessories to the product line. He built a new headquarters shaped like a giant basket, new company buildings, and a state-of-the-art childcare facility for employees' children. But Longaberger wasn't finished—he saw the need to lure tourists into the East Central Ohio area—so he added a golf course nearby and began assembling Longaberger Homestead, a shopping area with restaurants and entertainment near his hometown of Dresden, Ohio.

Dave Longaberger's failures were inconsequential compared to his decisive successes. His legacy includes community involvement, generosity, and the ability to resuscitate a depressed area, as well as making baskets and a buck or two. He commented, "What gives me the greatest pleasure is having the ability to make a difference in people's lives." His company is recognized as one of the most generous companies in America.

Fear of Self

Some people fear making decisions outside of their area of expertise. Feeling one-dimensional, they paste a "Good at Only One Thing" label on themselves, completely ignoring the varied abilities they have and their ability to learn and grow. Such narrow thinking makes a computer whiz incapable of deciding on a vacation destination. Or a guy who knows every baseball player's batting average unable to remember his wife's dress size because he distrusts his fashion sense.

Jack Kahl originally bought the company he named Manco Inc., because it was small and manageable, something he could safely handle. As the company grew, he panicked:

> I started reading books on it and started pretending to others that I was capable of [leading a big company], even though I didn't believe it on the inside. Now it's easy to share that because now I know I can do it. But in 1981, I didn't think so. I was looking like it, talking like it, acting like it, but I didn't believe it for a minute.

When his finance person resigned because Manco's books were six months in arrears, Kahl remembers:

> I was completely broken in spirit because I thought I had bankrupted. It was far worse in my mind than it was in reality....I held myself responsible for being so stupid that I had not seen it coming. It was the darkest single moment of

> my existence. I lost a great deal of confidence in myself and my judgment. I got some counseling and found out a lot of people go through what I did. Slowly, ever so slowly, I started rebuilding a little faith in myself.

Earlier Kahl had developed a habit of hiring friends whenever he needed business advice. He worked his way out of this situation by being decisive:

> The need to bring in people from professional service areas who could see the big picture became obvious to me....I had to break relationships to do that. I had to ask others to step aside and act as advisers rather than doers. I kept the friendships but changed the people who did the business. So there was a lot of emotional stuff going on. I pulled through by reading, trying, and not quitting. That was the biggest thing.

Jack Kahl's very honest description of his fears shows that it is possible to overcome fear and become decisive enough to salvage a company and a career. Manco CEO Kahl demonstrates that we are limited more by our thoughts than our actual abilities.

Fear of Looking Foolish

Decision-makers are allowed to look foolish, to stop being overly serious about life, and to take a little time to play. Albert Einstein wrote that the freedom to play with ideas and concepts is a vital source of creativity. If Einstein didn't mind looking foolish, who are we to feel self-conscious?

In 1948 the first instant camera hit the stores; demonstrators showed off Polaroid Land Camera Model 95 for $89.75. Nearby in the display counter, Kodak's Baby Brownie was priced at only $2.75. Would people snicker and walk away or be enthralled by the more expensive new technology? Would Polaroid's management look foolish or like marketing geniuses? The entire stock—56 Polaroids per store—was gone at the end of the day.

In 1914 Henry Ford took a calculated chance of looking foolish when he raised the salary of his assembly line workers to $5 a day. This enabled workers to buy better houses, more clothes, and maybe even take exotic vacations. Instead, they did what Ford figured they would do—they bought cars. By making sure that his workers could afford to buy his product, Ford created a market for Fords.

In 1981 Jan Carlzon was the new chief of SAS airline; he sent 10,000 front-line managers to two-day seminars and 25,000 managers for three-week courses designed to improve their job performance. Critics saw this as a foolish waste of money; supporters viewed it as an investment in employees' morale. Within four months, SAS was the most punctual European airline and its service levels were rejuvenated. How I wish today's airline CEOs would risk looking this foolish!

Fear of the Unknown

Fear of being intimidated by uncertain results keeps people from making marvelous discoveries. Think of Meriwether Lewis and William Clark and their 19th-century expedition into the American Northwest. Okay, so maybe that's a little extreme, but how about this everyday example provided by writer Donna Rae Smith:

> When Victor Ide, a Wal-Mart executive, met David Black, a deaf man, he hesitated to be his friend because there were so many unknowns. Ide's mother was deaf and he could use sign language, but he still feared making a fool of himself. What could he and Black have in common? Somehow, Ide got beyond his fears and risked trying to communicate with Black. As their friendship grew, Ide grew as a person and as a manager; he took advanced sign language classes and began hiring people with physical disabilities. Recognizing his own disability—fear of the unknown—Ide was no longer afraid to bring disabled people into the workplace.

The unknown is simply something that you have not learned about yet; that in itself is neither good or bad, just unknown. As I always remind people, if you have one foot on the dock and one foot in the boat, you're not going anywhere. The only way to get somewhere is to decisively paddle out into the unknown.

Fear of Change

Just because something is familiar does not mean that it cannot be improved on. Our bodies, for example, are constantly changing; new cells are created to replace those that die. Our minds are constantly learning, exchanging old ideas for new ones. Our world is changing faster than it ever has before; even though we cannot keep up with all the changes, we can decide which ones we want to monitor.

A retired officer of an oil company, Frank Mosier, recalled that when he was a company CEO, he thought he had all the answers. Gradually, he began to realize that he was not getting any smarter or more creative, so he invited workers, supervisors, and middle managers to suggest ways their work could be better organized. The workers responded with an overwhelming number of ideas; however, their supervisors and middle managers became defensive. They thought they should be the ones pitching their workers' ideas to top management. Mosier disagreed because he believed workers who received no credit for their ideas would not be motivated to improve their workplace.

Another example of a quick change: In 1959 when it brought its big motorbikes to America, Honda found that customers were unhappy about the bikes' performance. Ironically, buyers flocked to see the little Supercub bikes that Honda's managers used. Deciding to change direction, Honda started selling the Supercubs and changed the motorbike business almost overnight.

Solve Problems Now

Common sense tells us that we should solve our problems immediately, because festering problems only get more aggravating. As Ann Landers has pointed out, if we are angry with someone and keep thinking about that person, we are letting someone live in our brains rent-free. That image alone should help you make decisions so you can to evict all the freeloaders.

Let's say you were promised an interesting job but for the last year the work has been so repetitious that you hate going to work. You need to take action to solve this problem.

- First, decide what could happen and figure out how you are going to react in each case. Decide what you are going to say to your supervisor ahead of time; rehearse your side of the story. This isn't the time to be disgruntled, angry, hostile, blaming, or threatening.

- ➢ Second, ask for an appointment to talk with your immediate supervisor.
- ➢ Third, once you have an appointment, go in prepared to listen and communicate. Explain why you are unhappy or bored with your job. Ask what you can do to change the situation. Remain calm and cool.

If you misunderstood what the job entailed and the supervisor cannot do anything to help you, you have more decisions to make. Should you look for another job? Transfer to another job in the same company? Go back to school for additional training?

If your actions have caused the supervisor to narrow the job's scope, find out how you can improve. Mention that once you take the appropriate actions, you would like some feedback from the supervisor so you can be sure you are on the right track.

If your boss tells you that other people have caused the problem, ask what can be done to remedy the situation. The key here is not to let the situation take on a life of its own. Then you'll overreact and complain to co-workers, which creates an oppressive, stressful workplace. Taking action is empowering; complaining to your co-workers is a waste of time.

Journal Notes About Being Decisive: Developing the Qualities of Success

Look within to discover the fears that can keep you from making good decisions, or any decisions at all. Which fears keep you from taking action? Write down these fears and the reasons you have them:

FEAR: ______________________________

____

____

REASONS FOR THIS FEAR:

____

____

____

____

FEAR: ______________________________

____

____

REASONS FOR THIS FEAR:

____

____

____

____

FEAR: ______________________________

____

____

REASONS FOR THIS FEAR:

____

____

____

____

Reflect on decisions you have made recently and describe the process you used in reaching each decision. Mention how long you took to reach each decision and tell how the decision turned out.

DECISION: ______________________________

____

PROCESS: ______________________________

____

____

____

TIME: ______________

RESULT: ______________________________

____

DECISION: ______________________________

____

PROCESS: ______________________________

____

____

____

TIME: ______________

RESULT: ______________________________

____

DECISION: ______________________________

____

PROCESS: ______________________________

____

____

____

TIME: ______________

RESULT: ______________________________

____

Chapter 6

Focused

When Stefanie Spielman learned that she had breast cancer, her husband had to choose between his two obsessions—football and family. That decision turned out to be a no-brainer; four-time Pro Bowl linebacker Chris Spielman opted to sit out the 1998 season to care for his wife and family instead of playing for the Buffalo Bills. Known as a hard worker who played with determination, Spielman focused his tenacious winning spirit on helping his wife recover. He even shaved his head while Stefanie went through chemotherapy.

During her recovery, Stefanie frequently spoke to women's groups about the importance of having breast exams; the Spielmans made personal appearances to raise more than $237,000 for breast cancer research in 1998. By late 1999, the Spielmans had reached their goal of $1 million for breast cancer research.

Once his wife had recovered, Spielman returned to the gridiron as a Cleveland Brown for the 1999 season. During a preseason game, for the first time in his life, Spielman was helped off the field. For several seconds he was not been able to move his arms or legs due to a neck injury. Once again, he had to choose; this time between being healthy for the family he loved and incurring possible paralysis due to injuries while playing the sport he loved. Spielman chose his family.

Chris Spielman has made a career out of hanging tough in gut-wrenching situations, but none were as difficult as the two just described. Anyone watching from the sidelines could tell that Spielman values being a husband, a father, a family man; he also values being successful at whatever he does. In this chapter, we look at focusing on value-based priorities, ways to determine your priorities, and successful people like Chris Spielman who focus on what is important to them.

Identify Your Values

By looking within you can identify which values are really meaningful to you; then you can set priorities to achieve those values. At some point, people who haven't identified their values are forced to do so by a crisis, trauma, or catastrophe that brings them up short and makes them decide what they truly value.

I often ask my audiences, "When do most people take time to recognize the value of good health?" Without fail they answer, "When they're sick." Then I remind them that many times people would not have gotten sick if they had identified the value of being healthy and set some priorities for maintaining good health.

When a crisis caused by chest pains, a sore that won't heal, or a constant pain sends people to their doctors, they realize that health is an important value. Recognizing a truly meaningful value, such as health, causes them to accomplish the priorities that they set. For instance, smokers would focus on ways to stop smoking if they valued being healthy and wanted to quit smoking to achieve that goal.

One of my own values is to be healthy because I want to enjoy being alive for as long as I live. My priorities supporting this value are to eat healthy meals and to run regularly; focusing on health makes me run even when I'd rather relax at the beach. Another of my values is to help other people; my priorities are to help children through Make-A-Wish and to use the talent God has given me to help people be successful. When I was a manager I valued being successful in my career; two of my priorities were to be responsive to my employees and to meet my deadlines. By looking within, I recognized these values, set priorities for them, and focused on them.

Often when I am working with young people, they comment that they do not know how to even begin to identify their values. So, I suggest that they think about people they look up to and thoroughly admire and then decide why these people are admirable. For example, when a guy mentioned that a teacher always looked nice and was honest and straightforward with him, I stopped him right there to point out that he had just named three of his values: attractiveness, honesty, and directness.

Clearly, thinking about what you do not like about some people is another way to determine your own values; for example, if you dislike power-hungry dictators, you may value using your power to help others. Similarly, if you value humility, you won't want to be around those who are bragging constantly; if you value patience, you'll avoid impatient people.

As I mentioned in the Introduction, writing down your values and priorities is a must; it's like engraving them on your brain. You'll have a chance to do some engraving on your brain at the end of this chapter.

Motivational speaker Brian Tracy agrees with the need to write down priorities or goals and takes it one step further. Tracy promises that even doing the minimum—writing down 10 goals for the coming year and then not looking at them until 12 months later—will cause you to make progress toward those priorities. Of course, he's right, but just imagine how much better you can do if you focus on ways to achieve what you want! Remember the last time you drove right by a freeway exit because you were too busy singing along with your favorite CD? That's what happens when we lose focus; we get to our destination eventually. But why take the long way?

Focus on Your Value-Based Priorities

Priorities are part dream, part struggle, part expectation, and part discipline. Dreams are the most motivating part of all priorities. The dream causes you to expect whatever you desire when you look within; even when your dream changes through the years, your expectation remains strong. The struggle results from your knowledge that you must work to achieve your dream; and discipline causes you to focus on keeping your value-based priorities on track each day.

Former NASA mission controller Gene Kranz understands the power of dreams. Recently he said that space travel is important because it makes us dream and then stretch ourselves to accomplish those dreams. Kranz also commented: "If we can teach young people to dream, and to keep that dream ever in front of them, always aiming high, and never surrendering that dream, then we have a future as a nation."

After identifying your values, you can set priorities by looking within at each facet of your life. Just where is your job or career headed? Is your family's cohesiveness developing or crumbling? Exactly what possibilities do you see in your community? Is your own personal growth a priority for you? Do you value your circle of friends or take everyone for granted? Is your religion a daily conversation with your Higher Power or a ritual restricted to weekends?

Such questions are just the beginning of those that you need to ask and answer to establish priorities; the best time to establish priorities is when you finish reading this chapter. If you are serious about being successful, write down your values and priorities for each major part of your life. This will help you to keep focused on what you are doing.

Speaking of focusing, Jack Canfield, who developed the *Chicken Soup* series of books with Mark Victor Hansen, mentioned in a recent speech that one of the most difficult things for all of us today is to stay focused because there's just too much stuff going on. To prove it, he told this story: While instructing a young monk, the director of novices mentioned that one of the hardest things the young monk would have to do was to stay very focused because staying focused is difficult for most people. The young monk answered that that wouldn't be a problem, regardless of whether he was praying or working. The older monk smiled and reassured him that staying focused would be a big problem. Then he paused and said, "I'll tell you what. If you can say the Our Father from beginning to end without an interruption, and stay focused on what you are saying, I'll give you my horse."

The young monk's eyes opened wide in amazement and he said slowly, "You're going to give me your horse just for saying the Our Father?" The older monk nodded, "Absolutely, you say the Our Father from beginning to end without interruption and stay focused on what you are saying and I'll give you my horse."

The young monk answered, "I can do that, I'm ready to go." He took a deep breath and started: "Our Father who art in heaven, hallowed be thy name, thy would that include the saddle?"

Choose Reasonable Priorities

Deciding on specific priorities can be impossible if you expect to be perfect, or to set priorities based on others' values. Also, you may find it hard to give up something, to change, or to take a chance. For example, when I was 16, I valued my very first car, a 1955 Chevy, which was tied into ego, my value of looking good, and my self-esteem. Accordingly, one of my highest priorities was keeping that car in running shape and looking great to attract all the beautiful cheerleaders. I washed that car a minimum of three times a week.

Today, I still value my car but my priorities are to keep it reasonably clean and running well. Obviously, my car is no longer my number-one value. Today I don't care if my car is spotless or bigger than anyone else's car. My values have changed and with them my priorities. Becoming a family man—or woman—can have a major impact on a list of values. Because your priorities change as your values change, reviewing your values and reassessing your priorities becomes a constant, ongoing way to focus on success.

In 1993, rap artist M. C. Hammer released his first album; one of the tunes on that album was "Can't Touch This," an overnight hit that was played on every station and used in commercials. Hammer sold more than 5 million albums in a very short time; he made $33 million, so he went from having very little to being a multimillionaire. Hammer began spreading his money around; he built a huge home and hired 200 people.

In the summer of 1999, Dr. Nancy Snyderman of ABC-TV interviewed Hammer; she asked how he could possibly lose $33 million and have 200 people working for him. "What would you say was your biggest mistake?" she asked. Hammer replied, "I'll tell you one thing, I was moving around to too many things and I was not focused. I didn't prioritize the things I needed to prioritize and stay focused on one thing at a time."

Choose the Doable, Not Perfection

When choosing priorities, you need to consider what is possible, probable, or improbable. For instance, you may have as a value making your community a place where the golden rule reigns. Is it possible? Yes, but is it probable or improbable? Although an overnight change may be improbable, a gradual change could be probable. You may want to break down the elements of a golden rule community, and set priorities for each element. This is what Sammy Lee did when he practiced his gold-medal skill.

Sammy Lee

In the 1920s many in Fresno, Calif. disliked the increasing number of Asians moving into town. The Lees came from Korea. Because his father taught him that hard work could change others' false opinions of them, Lee set two goals for himself: to be a doctor and to be the world's best diver. Although some of his friends told Lee his second goal was impossible, Lee was certain he had gold-medal talent.

After serving in World War II, Lee enrolled at the University of Southern California Medical School and set up a tough diving practice schedule for himself. Following graduation, Lee earned a place on the U.S. Olympic team. In 1948 he won a gold medal for high diving, now called platform diving.

Four years later, Lee won a second gold medal for high diving. In addition to becoming an ear, nose, and throat specialist, Lee coached promising young divers. During the 1970s and 80s, Lee coached U.S. diver Greg Louganis, who won two gold medals for platform diving. Through the years, Lee's life has been intertwined with the Olympics; in 1990 he was elected to the U.S. Olympic Hall of Fame. Sammy Lee established his priorities early in life and did not let anything stand in his way—even the seemingly impossible.

Make It a Stretch

Just as Sammy Lee did, you can stretch yourself to reach your priority. Betting the farm on one of your values, such as being a success, takes courage, luck, and persistence—in other words, being a pretty special person who must be successful. For instance, if your value is to be as rich as Bill Gates, founder of Microsoft, your priority is to come up with a billion-dollar idea. Although setting priorities focuses your energies, it does not create something from nothing. If your career priority has dollar signs and you are still looking for a billion-dollar idea, start lower and ratchet the figure up each year. Start with someone lower on the billionaire list and work your way up. The psychology behind this approach is that focused baby steps help you see that change is possible. So go ahead and focus on the stars, knowing that your slim chance means you'll have to work twice as hard. That's what James Wong Howe did.

James Wong Howe

Not long after his birth in China, Howe's father brought him to Pasco, Wash. As the only Chinese person in his school, Howe learned to fight early on; Howe was so skillful with his fists that he was asked to leave school. Howe complied and went on the road, billing himself as the only Chinese fighter in the United States. He fought throughout the Northwest and down the coast to California.

While watching a Mack Sennett comedy being filmed in Los Angeles, Howe changed his career value from being a boxer to becoming a cameraman. His first priority to achieve that value was buying a camera so he could begin taking pictures and experimenting. Howe's second priority was to work steadily, which he eventually did after receiving a studio contract.

By the 1940s Howe was the best-paid cameraman in Hollywood. Throughout his career he worked on 119 feature films, was nominated for 16 Academy Awards, and won for *The Rose Tattoo* and for *Hud*. Other well-known Howe films include *Casablanca*; *Come Back, Little Sheba*; and *The Old Man and the Sea*.

Despite being one of the greatest cinematographers and having worked in America all of his life, James Howe could not become a U.S. citizen until 1952, when Congress passed the McCarran-Walter Act that allowed foreign-born immigrants to become citizens.

Be Able to Give Something Up

When we are children, we see things as all or nothing. Fortunately, as we grow wiser, we learn that sometimes by giving something up, or by changing a situation, we get what we want. Say, for example, you value living in a dry house near a babbling brook. Because you already live close to a babbling brook that turns into a torrent of muddy water every spring, you have little chance of remaining dry. So you focus on how to achieve your value—a dry house near a babbling brook—by choosing between possible priorities, both of which require giving up something: spending money to elevate your house on stilts to keep it dry, or giving up the sound of the babbling brook by moving your house to higher ground.

Gene Kranz

A few years ago I was one of the morning speakers during a three-day program for Century 21 in Las Vegas; later that evening, I was fortunate enough to hear former NASA flight director Gene Kranz's keynote address, during which he discussed how our dreams help us focus on our priorities. The biggest challenge of his life, Gene Kranz admitted, was to finish high school, so he could get on with his dream. Kranz recalled, "I didn't like school. I did poorly in school. All I wanted to do was fly." While attending high school, he was not a good student and spent most of his time at a small airfield where he did odd jobs and learned to fly. It seems that Kranz's values were freedom and doing something unique.

At some point he realized that to make aviation his career (a value) he would have to focus on math, physics, and chemistry (priorities). In other words, Kranz had to give up some of his time at the airfield and turn it into study time. After receiving a college degree in aeronautical engineering, Kranz became a jet fighter pilot, a flight-test engineer, and a NASA mission controller. He is best known, perhaps, as the flight director who brought crippled *Apollo 13* back from the moon.

Set Priorities Only for Yourself

No one can expect to see results for priorities that they set for someone else. Someone who owns a small business, for example, may expect her son to carry on the business, but that priority is one her son must choose. Dreams collide when we focus on forcing our priorities on others. Give only pep talks to others, and focus on priorities only for yourself.

Choose to Change Your Behavior

If being more patient with your family is a value, start by setting priorities to curb your impatience. Adopting a priority of counting to 10 before responding still works, but sometimes counting to 50 is more realistic. Also consider how your impatience affects others. For instance, if your impatience stems mainly from a lack of time and the pressure of other things you must do, each evening, make family time a priority so your family feels that they are the most important thing in your life. Focus your energies on them during these hours rather than thinking about anything else you could be doing. Show them how much you value them.

Review Your Values and Then Prioritize

Whether it's once a month, once every six months, or once a year, how often you review your values and priorities is up to you. I always say, the more often you look within and ask "How am I doing?" the better. This is especially true when you feel stuck, like you're not going anywhere. That's when you should review your journal to see how far you have come, and when you will appreciate the whole series of baby steps that enabled you to focus on your priorities and live what you value.

Whenever we make changes, we run the risk of getting stuck or impatient. If your priority involves a sea of changes in your life, you may find the slowness of change is unnerving—just remember that baby steps count.

I thought about baby steps when I visited the Cape Hatteras Lighthouse, 208 feet of seacoast history in North Carolina, not too long before they moved it back from the coast. Once this 4,800-ton lighthouse warned ships away from the treacherous waters off Cape Hatteras. Despite being replaced by modern technology, the lighthouse has become part of America's heritage; because it was threatened by coastal erosion, contractors moved the lighthouse 2,900 feet inland in 1999. After being propped up on rollers, the brick tower's first move was all of five inches. Engineers said that even on the best days, they could move it fewer than 200 feet at a time—less than the length of a football field. The move took three weeks but it would not have mattered if it took three months. The important part is that they successfully moved the lighthouse to a better location. Similarly, baby steps can lead you to a better place.

Like moving the Cape Hatteras Lighthouse, your priorities may not be achieved as quickly as you wish, but stay focused; they are definitely worth pursuing—even an inch at a time.

Maurice Ashley

The only black chess grandmaster of 470 grandmasters worldwide, Ashley values his wife and daughter, his community center for chess players in Harlem, N.Y., his Web site, his chess CD, playing chess, and teaching chess.

With the exception of his family, all of these values have priorities that focus on his original value—mastering chess. When Ashley was 14, another 14-year-old beat him at chess. Because that had never happened before, it got Ashley's attention. His priority became to learn all he could about chess. He began reading about chess. Then, after defeating his opponent who had won earlier, Ashley kept learning and playing chess. Next, he added a new value—coaching young players in Harlem, because chess develops their concentration, focus, problem solving, and goal setting. He coached students in Harlem from 1989 to 1997, when he devoted himself to competition. It took two years of chess playing to accumulate a 2,600 performance rating; that's when he became a grandmaster. All together, his value of becoming a world-class chess player took 20 years of focused effort.

Plan Your Day

Do you have to? Absolutely, if you want to keep focused on your priorities in the midst of back-to-back meetings, or even the minutiae and pressures of daily life. Planning your day can be as simple as looking within and writing what you want to accomplish that day on an index card. At the end of the day, take a look and congratulate yourself for what you accomplished. If some items were not done, figure out why and how to avoid the same thing happening again. Using this learning process is a quick way to find out what is distracting you from focusing on your value-based priorities.

Many times a problem item is something you really do not want to do, so try doing that first. For instance, if you hate dental checkups, request your dentist's first appointment of the day. Or, if you value getting healthy but lack the time, set your alarm clock 20 minutes earlier and assemble your running gear so it's the first thing you see when the alarm clock rings. Remember that running two blocks is better than staying in bed, especially when you plan to run three blocks the following week. Taking focused baby steps at first brings you closer to your value of getting healthy.

Dustin's Mom

A few years ago, while waiting for a storm-delayed flight to take me to Colorado Springs for a speaking engagement at the

U.S. Air Force Academy, I was hanging out in the Denver airport. Leaning against one of the pillars, I watched people passing by.

A young lady walked by rather briskly with a little guy just about 4 years of age running beside her. As she went by, she glanced over at me, slowed down, and stopped about 20 feet past me. Glancing back, she turned and walked back toward me slowly. Then she turned and continued on her way, stopped again, turned around and stared at me. By this time, I'm wondering what's not zippered or buttoned. I should mention that when I'm not speaking to groups, I don't shave, I wear shorts, and I let my hair get messy. That day at the airport, I had a 5-day-old beard and was wearing shorts and a sweatshirt under a ski jacket.

The young lady came back, stood right in front of me, and said, "I know who you are! You're Tom Bay! You look like Tom Bay. Aren't you Tom Bay? You look a little different. Aren't you Tom Bay?"

As I nodded, she continued: "You see this little guy? I want you to meet him, his name is Dustin. I wanted to tell you I attended a time-management seminar you gave about a year and a half ago. It was wonderful—more about life management than just using a calendar or book. About 90 minutes into the program you talked about values, about the lack of priorities, and the lack of time available for our true values. And with that you recited 'Cat's in the Cradle.'"

"Yes," I said, "I use 'Cat's in the Cradle' in almost all of my talks."

She said, "I'll never forget that refrain:

> 'When you coming home dad?'
> 'I can't say when, but we'll have a good time then.'

"And then the father called his grown son who didn't have time to even talk. It really hit home and right afterward you said, 'Our lives tick off one second at a time.' I'll never forget you saying that. Looking around the room I saw how many women were biting their lips, and the men were looking down at their shoes. I was thinking to myself in a rather egotistical way, well I know one thing, I'm not a 'Cat's in the Cradle' mom.

"Well, Tom, the insight that I had really showed up the following day during our morning circus. I have two sons—11 and 12 years old. Dustin here was a little bit of a surprise, but a wonderful surprise." She paused to beam at her fidgety son.

"I have a job and my husband has his own company. Each morning we're busy getting our older sons off to school and making sure they've got their homework and lunch money. I always warn them to come home right after school so they're there when I call to check on them. Then I say goodbye. Meanwhile, I'm trying to clean up the dishes and get myself out the door. With all of this commotion, Dustin comes over one day and starts tugging on my skirt and I said, 'Just a minute, dear,' because my husband is going out the door saying, 'Honey, I love you. Don't forget the meeting we have tonight.'

"When they were all gone, I finally looked down as I'm finishing up with the dishes and said, 'Yes, honey, what do you want?'

"'Mommy, mommy, ya wanna color?' and he's standing there holding up his coloring book and crayons. At this point I said, 'Not now, honey, mommy's too...too....' And the word busy stuck in my throat. And I thought to myself, how often have I said to this young man, I'm too busy? And yet, I'm not a 'Cat's in the Cradle' mom. When Dustin's baby-sitter showed up, I gave my son a hug as I left. Tom, I got maybe a half a block away and all of it welled up inside of me. I'm thinking of all the things I'm doing, and I don't have time to color. I served on four boards of directors and I chaired two of them. I did volunteer work for three or four groups because it's good for my husband's business. I tried to exercise a couple or three times a week. I did so many things, but I didn't have time to color.

"Tom, I'm so glad that I've have a chance to tell you this: Today, I serve on one board and that is by choice. I refused to chair that board, but I chose to serve on it. I do volunteer work for one organization that I chose. I'm an outstanding mom and wife. I do exercise and take good care of my health. All these are by choice. And, today I have time to color, and that's my choice."

That five or six minutes in the airport was one of the most motivational talks that I have ever heard. When my pace gets frantic, I remind myself to take time to color. And I ask myself if my actions reflect my values and whether my priorities are in order or if I need to reprioritize. I ask myself what's truly important in my life and whether I am focusing on it. And then, I take time to color.

Journal Notes About Being Focused: Developing the Qualities of Success

It's time to commit to some priorities for the things you value. First, write down your values in the following spaces. Second, fill in the priorities that will help you to achieve them. Third, rank your values by placing the number 1 on the line to the left of your most important values, 2 to the left of the second most important values, and so on.

As you focus on each priority based on your values for 20 days, write about what worked and what did not. Also, describe what you learned about your ability to focus on each specific priority.

FAMILY VALUE: ______________________________

MY PRIORITIES FOR MY FAMILY:

1. ______________________________
2. ______________________________
3. ______________________________

WHAT WORKED:

____

____

____

WHAT DID NOT WORK:

____

____

____

I LEARNED:

____

____

____

Work or Career Value: ______________________

My Priorities for My Work or Career:

1. ______________________
2. ______________________
3. ______________________

What Worked:

____

____

____

What Did Not Work:

____

____

I Learned:

____

____

Personal Growth Value: ______________________

My Priorities for My Personal Growth:

1. ______________________
2. ______________________
3. ______________________

What Worked:

____

____

____

What Did Not Work:

____

____

I Learned:

____

____

FRIENDSHIP VALUE: ____

MY PRIORITIES FOR MY FRIENDS:

1. ____

2. ____

3. ____

WHAT WORKED:

____

____

____

WHAT DID NOT WORK:

____

____

I LEARNED:

____

____

RELIGIOUS VALUE: ____

MY PRIORITIES FOR MY RELIGION:

1. ____

2. ____

3. ____

WHAT WORKED:

____

____

____

WHAT DID NOT WORK:

____

____

I LEARNED:

____

____

CITIZENSHIP VALUE: ______________________________

MY PRIORITIES FOR MY COMMUNITY:

1. ______________________________

2. ______________________________

3. ______________________________

WHAT WORKED:

____

____

____

WHAT DID NOT WORK:

____

____

I LEARNED:

____

____

Chapter 7

Visionary

Summers in the 1950s should have been carefree for children—filled with swimming pools, lemonade stands, matinees at air-conditioned theaters, pickup ball games, and new friends. Many U.S. parents, however, made their children stay away from pools, movie theaters, and kids they didn't know. Frightened by a poliomyelitis epidemic, some parents even blamed air-conditioning—a fairly recent invention—because no one really knew why so many children contracted polio in the summertime. Despite parents' safeguards, 60,000 children contracted polio in one year at the height of the epidemic.

In 1954 Dr. Jonas Salk developed a vaccine containing dead polio viruses that partially stopped the epidemic; an unfortunate side effect of these shots was that inoculated children could become carriers of polio. Meanwhile, Dr. Albert Sabin saw the need for a longer-lasting solution and created an oral vaccine containing three strains of polio virus that were weakened, but alive. Taking an amazing risk that could have meant death, paralysis, or life in an iron lung, Dr. Sabin tried the vaccine on himself. When he had no ill effects, Sabin tried it on prison volunteers. In 1960 Sabin's oral vaccine with its more powerful immune response ended polio epidemics in the United States. Later the Sabin vaccine was instrumental in eliminating polio in other countries.

Until 2000, U.S. doctors inoculated youngsters with both vaccines even though about eight inoculated children developed polio annually due to a side effect of the Sabin oral vaccine. Now doctors use only the Salk shots to inoculate children against polio. Elsewhere in the world, the Sabin oral vaccine is still the vaccine of choice for mass vaccination campaigns to control outbreaks of wild poliovirus.

Before developing the oral polio vaccine, Albert Sabin had developed vaccines against dengue fever and Japanese encephalitis, so he had a successful track record, yet this visionary risked something that few of us would face—death. This chapter looks at visionaries who see possibilities and take risks to achieve them.

Being Courageous, Fearless, and Bold

Today we are fortunate enough to be surrounded by visionaries. Everywhere we look, we see people with vision, including:

- Dikembe Mutombo, Atlanta Hawks center, who is building a $44 million hospital in his homeland, the Democratic Republic of the Congo.
- Irish Protestants and Catholics who are working for a lasting peace in Ireland after decades of hate and murder.
- Rosie O'Donnell has donated $4.7 million to children's causes, yet she accepts no credit for her charitable works. She claims that she has more than enough money and that the real heroes are the mothers working their way out of welfare.

Sociologist Ashley Montagu once illustrated one of his talks by showing a film of a child learning how to stand; later the child crawled around exploring its environment. This child was utterly joyful, curious, open, experimental, playful, and sensitive. Montagu reminded his audience that we are all designed to be like that child—courageous, fearless, and bold. In other words, we all start out as visionaries.

Once we grow up, however, only about half of us are still fearless and bold. Most grownups feel strongly about taking risks—they either like or dislike it—very few people are indifferent to risks. The nothing-ventured-nothing-gained crowd actually prefers risky situations; unfortunately, they may expose themselves, others, or their organizations to unnecessary risks. When facing a risk, they:

- Underestimate the uncertainties.
- Are overly optimistic when taking action.
- Seek excitement and novelty.
- Overestimate the probability of attaining what they want.
- Make decisions impulsively.

The better-safe-than-sorry group never saw a risk they couldn't avoid; therefore, they also avoid opportunities to influence the outcomes they desire. When facing a risk, they

- ➢ Overestimate the uncertainties.
- ➢ Defer taking action due to being overly pessimistic.
- ➢ Prefer security and comfort.
- ➢ Underestimate or ignore the probability of attaining the desired outcomes.
- ➢ Postpone making decisions or give up too quickly.

Both groups need to look within to become real visionaries. The risk lovers need to realize that some risks just aren't worth taking. They need to balance the thrill of taking risks with how the outcome could affect themselves and others.

Those in the risk-averse group need to develop successful risk-taking track records. Dr. John Travis, a wellness expert, suggests that instead of fearing to take a risk we trisk, by combining trust and risk. Each time risk-averse persons take risks and are successful, they trust themselves a bit more, mentally, emotionally, and spiritually. Like visionaries, they can take calculated risks that increase their ability to accept risks as part of life.

Fulfill Your Vision

Roland Hayes had a vision; even while he was risking everything, he trusted that his talent would eventually ensure his success. The son of ex-slaves, Roland Hayes was the first black man to win wide acclaim as a concert artist. In 1916 Hayes wanted to give his first solo concert but no one would sponsor him. Everyone he talked to was convinced that a black man could not understand European classical music, and that even if he could, no one would pay to hear him sing. Undaunted by the naysayers, Hayes spent his life's savings—everything he had earned as a page at a life insurance company—to rent Boston's Jordan Hall. Hayes lost every penny of his investment.

The following year, Hayes again announced he would give a concert, and again no one offered to sponsor him. Using all of the money he received while touring black churches and colleges, he rented Boston's Symphony Hall. After mailing concert announcements to more than 3,000 people, Hayes had tickets printed and sold them himself. On the evening of November 15, 1917, when Hayes stepped onto the stage, there wasn't an empty seat in the house; in fact, 700 people had to be turned away. As Roland Hayes demonstrated, taking a calculated risk rooted in a vision is an important part of our lives.

Take Risks Willingly

Marg Geller received a "genius grant" from the MacArthur Foundation in 1990. A cosmologist, she studies the nature of the universe, which she is mapping. Geller is convinced that our willingness to take risks is very important. As a scientist, she naturally speaks of risk-taking in science; however, what she says applies equally to all areas of life: Risks are gifts to be used.

> The willingness to take risks is very important in science. If you don't take any risks, you'll never do anything having real impact. Never. That's very hard to learn because people always advise you to take the more secure job position, for example. It's not good advice because security doesn't really matter. If you're going to do creative things, you have to be secure in the idea that you can create. That's the only kind of security that actually matters. If you don't have that you don't have anything. Obviously you have to make a living, but if you are genuinely creative, you will make a living. It's extremely hard to learn that because it requires an enormous inner strength.

Risking Conviction

In 1942 three men willingly risked their freedom for their principles, for their vision of democracy; as Geller suggests, their actions had a real impact. In April of that year General John L. DeWitt issued an order that all people of Japanese ancestry—even those who were American citizens—were under curfew and should prepare to leave for detention camps. Most Japanese thought the best way to help the country was to obey, but not all Japanese.

Gordon Hirabayashi of Seattle was a student at the University of Washington. At first he followed the curfew rule, but then he reread the Bill of Rights and found proof that he could not be singled out because he was Japanese. So Hirabayashi ignored the curfew and was jailed.

Minoru Yasui was a lawyer in Portland, Ore., whose legal training told him that the curfew and internment orders were against the law. He asked one of his friends to report to the police that he was violating the curfew. When ignored by the police, Yasui surrendered to them; he was fully prepared to use his $5,000 life savings to go to court.

Fred Korematsu refused to leave his Oakland, Calif., home for personal reasons. After being arrested, tried, and convicted, he was sent to prison.

In 1943 Hirabayashi appealed to the U.S. Supreme Court, which cited reasons of national safety and supported the Washington State court's decision. The Court also came to the same conclusion about Yasui's and Korematsu's convictions.

Four decades later, these three convictions were overturned by the Congressional Commission on Wartime Relocation and Internment of Civilians. This commission found the government had withheld information and misled the Supreme Court about the military necessity of relocation.

The legal battles of these three risk-taking visionaries helped document that racial discrimination, not national safety, was the reason for the internment of the Japanese-Americans. Accordingly, in 1988 Congress passed the Civil Liberties Act that authorized compensation for living survivors of the internment camps.

Taking Risks

Visionaries make decisions that have an uncertain potential for gain or loss; only rarely is the probability of gain or loss conclusive. The potential gains include money, health, power, respect, prestige, and positive relationships. The losses include the possibility of injury, liability, embarrassment, and wasted resources.

In studying how we take risks, psychologists Daniel Kahneman and Amos Tversky discovered that two behavior patterns affect our risk-taking:

1. The first behavior pattern occurs when emotion destroys the self-control that is essential to rational decision-making. For instance, someone considering jumping the Grand Canyon on a motorcycle may be attracted by the thrill factor and disregard the inherent danger.

The solution for thrill seekers is looking within and being aware of their own behavior patterns. Such self-awareness can keep the siren call of adventure from drowning out the danger of allowing emotions to overcome sense.

2. The second behavior pattern occurs when people are unable to understand fully what they are dealing with. Too often people with life-threatening illnesses fit this pattern; after hearing the diagnosis and possible treatments, they are overwhelmed and lack the ability to decipher the medical terminology.

Herbert Kindler suggests a solution for this problem: "The challenge is to respond after self-reflection and exploration, to prudently take risks that support productive change." Once again, looking within can provide the self-confidence to take calculated risks.

If you want to be a visionary success, you must be comfortable with taking risks. Whether you feel comfortable taking risks depends a lot on your personal experience, the culture of your family and workplace, your ethics, and your beliefs about personal responsibility. Despite these influences, if you are risk averse you can change by deciding that you want to be visionary and that some risk-taking is important to your personal success. Remember, fear is simply a **f**antasy **e**vent **a**ppearing **r**eal.

Take Challenging, Calculated Risks

Visionaries choose calculated risks that contain a good possibility of success. In a letter to his son, George Smith Patton, an American general affectionately known as Old Blood and Guts, advised: "Take calculated risks. That is quite different from being rash." Old Blood and Guts gave some good fatherly advice that not only helped his son understand risk-taking but also underscored a family tradition of taking calculated risks.

Years ago I owned a chain of men's stores and often had to calculate the risk factor of a business decision. Each time I asked myself what was the worst possible thing that could happen if nothing went right when I took that risk. I decided any risk that could cause me to lose my company was not worth it. Anytime taking a risk could set me back but not put me under, however, I would take that risk.

When I was in management, on my employees' first or second day on the job I always told them that I wanted them to feel comfortable enough to take risks. I also wanted them to feel comfortable enough to take the credit if the risk succeeded and to act accountably and responsibly if it failed.

One thing I learned was that taking a calculated risk sometimes means different things to various people due to the effects of cultural context and human psychology; thus, two people can look within themselves and come up with different reactions to the same calculated risk. Say, for example, two excellent employees are invited to apply for the same promotion. One may decline due to his family members' culture-dictated reluctance to brag about their abilities. The other person may go for it due to her family's tradition of always making the most of all opportunities.

Author Daniel Goleman stresses that leaders take calculated risks on the job. For instance, he found they won't ask for challenges they know they can't handle alone and they'll play on their own strengths. As an example, Goleman described this scenario:

> A midlevel employee...was invited to sit in on a strategy meeting with her company's top executives. Although she was the most junior person in the room, she did not sit there quietly, listening in awestruck or fearful silence. She knew she had a head for clear logic and the skill to present ideas persuasively, and she offered cogent suggestions about the company's strategy. At the same time, her self-awareness stopped her from wandering into territory where she knew she was weak.

Entrepreneurs

Classic risk-takers, entrepreneurs have always had the ability to see opportunities that the rest of us never notice. These visionaries have the knack of seeing how they can benefit from changes in society. They have found the risks of startups worth taking and have been taking calculated risks with new businesses for centuries. Lately a new breed of entrepreneurs has been meeting other people's need for more time. To bridge the gap created by people too busy to make cookies from scratch, several entrepreneurs armed with great cookie recipes have franchised their cookie stores. Today it's difficult to find a mall lacking the scent of freshly baked cookies or cinnamon buns.

Other entrepreneurs work on a smaller scale by planning and preparing family meals or dinner parties, shopping or running errands, taking the children to soccer practice and the clothes to the cleaners, throwing parties and cleaning up afterward, redecorating or cleaning homes, house and/or pet sitting, and even writing complaint letters. These people most likely started out by noticing a need, then they verified that fulfilling other people's needs would provide an enjoyable way to make a decent living or to start a franchise operation.

To Be Alive, Take Risks

Psychologist William James believed we need to take risks to feel alive: "It is only by risking our persons from one hour to another that we live at all. And often enough our faith beforehand in an uncertified result is the only thing that makes the result come true." In the next chapter we say more about the advantages of believing in personal luck.

Brother David Steindl-Rast, a lecturer/writer, agrees and believes risk taking is essential to achieve:

> To live is to take risks. It's absolutely central. Courage and risk are essential to aliveness. And aliveness is the thing that we all strive for and long for, yet sometimes barricade ourselves against out of fear...even as we are still longing for it. If we are not taking risks, it's still for the same reason that people do take risks, namely, we want to be alive. The ones who take risks because they want to come alive chose the correct way, while those who want to stay alive and so don't want to take risks chose the wrong way. But we all want the same thing.

Alive! That's probably how the signers of the Declaration of Independence felt in Philadelphia in 1776. Despite the heat, humidity, lack of ventilation, and argumentative nature of their group, these visionaries were embroiled in a gigantic, euphoric undertaking for which they would be known forever as heroes or fools. Such is the nature of taking risks.

In the 21st century, both politicians and entrepreneurs enjoy living on the edge; Richard Branson is an example of the latter.

Richard Branson

Striving for that alive feeling is not all bad when it is held in check. Richard Branson, the British billionaire who started Virgin Records and Virgin Atlantic Airlines, has made several attempts to circle the world in hot-air balloons. As a balloonist who holds several world records, Branson has an obvious appetite for risk. He also has respect for it: "In everything I do, I examine the downside, the danger, what can go wrong," he says. In fact, Branson bought just one plane when he started his airline: "And I had an agreement with Boeing to take it back if things didn't work out." Even though Branson has been phenomenally successful with the many and varied companies he has started, his never-on-time railroad has been an embarrassing disappointment to riders and owners alike. Undoubtedly he and his investors have learned a lot about what can go wrong.

U.S. Army

Entrepreneurs get used to risky, unfamiliar situations, and so do successful Army officers. According to Jack Miller, who leads the U.S. Army's program to select candidates for high command, "the Army operates a crude but effective filter to weed out people who can't tolerate risk: It moves them to new locations every few years. Those who can't adjust to novel situations eventually leave, and, you are left with a reasonably flexible officer corps."

James Forten

James Forten's life contained more risks than any one person should have. When he was only 14—but already 6'2"—he signed onto a rebel ship as a powder boy during the American Revolution. A second-generation free black, Forten was taking a tremendous risk, because the British routinely sold into slavery any blacks they captured. When his ship was captured, Forten was invited to join the Royal Navy but refused saying, "I am here as a prisoner for the liberties of my country. I cannot prove a traitor to her interests." That's a lot of risk-taking for a 14-year-old boy; he spent the rest of the war on a foul prison ship in New York harbor.

Forten later became a sail maker like his father and invented a hand-cranked winch to hoist sails. These enterprises enabled him to become the first black American millionaire. Visionary Forten was also the first civil rights leader and national spokesman for African-Americans. On a local level he made sure that black youngsters learned to read, write, and do arithmetic.

Newspaper headlines proclaimed the "Death of an Excellent Man" over articles describing the almost 5000 people who marched behind James Forten's coffin, "white and colored, male and female....Among the white portion were seen some of our wealthiest merchants and shippers, and captains of vessels." At that time, it was dangerous for whites to be seen with blacks on the streets of Philadelphia, but the merchants and shippers and captains of vessels didn't care—they had learned risk-taking from a visionary, James Forten.

Risking vs. Aging

The older some people get, the more comfortable their ruts become. Once they become comfortable, they don't want to take any risks; not changing is less stressful and doesn't frighten them the way risk-taking could. What a waste of talent and experience. Only visionaries risk not aging.

One way to take risks and still remain comfortable is by taking calculated risks, which reminds me of this story from Brother David Steindl-Rast: An elderly man lived in a tidy house with a steep wheelchair ramp leading down to the street. Every morning his neighbor watched the old fellow careen down the ramp in his wheelchair despite heavy traffic on the street. One day she cautioned him that speeding down that ramp was downright dangerous. Looking at her with bright, mischievous eyes, the old man answered, "Yesss, it is!" and laughed.

Learning from Failure

Some of the risks we take are not successful; even calculated risks can turn sour. When they do, it's time to look within and examine what went wrong; by finding the weak link in our logic, we can learn what not to do again. Bill Walsh, former coach of the NFL San Francisco 49ers, wrote: "The key to long-range success in sports—and in business—isn't how you deal with winning but how you deal with losing." Thus, as a visionary, you must not only accept the possibility of failure for any risk you take but also encourage those working for you to be comfortable with failure. If you are comfortable with failure, you can create a risk-taking, failure-accepting culture at your company and in your family.

When management consultant Naomi Karten was a CIO, she gave each of her employees two small and one large peel-and-stick dots with rules for their use. She recalled, "These allowed each person two small screw-ups and one outrageous screw-up during the course of a year." As long as they turned in the appropriate dot and told her what happened before anyone else did, employees were not in trouble. "It created a culture of 'nobody's perfect.' We can be human and still survive."

Author Tom Peters is certain that anyone working with the new technologies will fail from time to time: "If they're not failing, then they're not serious about the new technologies. Because nobody knows how all of this is going to sort itself out."

Proving Peters' statement, Barry Lynn, an executive vice president at Wells Fargo Bank, says that the bank "developed our Internet site three times before it worked right." In 1998 500,000 of the bank's 4 million customers were finally able to use online banking. While bank employees were taking risks and learning what would not work, they had Lynn's approval. Lynn believes there are two ways to fail:

1. Through stupid, uncaring failures where the person who failed should be punished, such as a car jockey in a garage who claims he knows how to drive a stick shift, but hasn't a clue.
2. Through a calculated risk or honest mistake, where valuable learning experiences result, such as hiring a painter who has excellent references, not realizing that his assistant would be doing your work.

Falling Forward

Lynn promotes risk-taking by making it clear that he and everyone else can live with failure. Lynn has created a falling forward program; its name illustrates that failing moves an individual or even an organization forward because learning accompanies failure. To spread the good word, each monthly Wells Fargo publication carries a story praising someone who has fallen forward.

Tom Finley, a human resources executive at Rubbermaid, suggests that employees' performance will be mediocre unless they are free to take risks and learn. "This is more critical in today's global marketplace where we are far more dependent on the initiative of people."

Trisk

Earlier I mentioned the need to trust your visionary abilities when you are taking a risk; at the same time, it is important that others trust you, too. When others are involved in a risk-taking project, be sure to keep everyone advised about how your project is going. Being honest and open creates trust and respect in those around you.

A good example is Eileen Strider, who was a CIO at Universal Underwriters Insurance Group. Strider hired an outside vendor to develop a system; a year later she canceled the $1 million project. During that year she had held weekly meetings about the project to establish trust. Each week she was truthful about how the project was going. She commented, "if the senior businessperson and my boss, the CEO, had not known me and known my intentions were good and I was trying very hard, I think they would have fired me."

I'll close this chapter with an idea from Wayne Gretzky, still the greatest hockey player ever, who knows about taking risks and has had the bruises to show for it. Gretsky says that 100 percent of all the shots you don't take don't go in. And Bay says, it's just the same for risks you don't take—they can't bring you success. So look within to pursue your vision and to find the courage to take risks.

Journal Notes About Being Visionary: Developing the Qualities of Success

Think about the risks you have taken during the past year. In the following section, describe each risk and how it affected you and others. Then continue to consider these risks and describe which influences (family, work, culture, ethics, and so on) guided your decision-making process for each. Also describe what you learned by taking each risk.

RISK: ____________________

EFFECT ON ME: ____________________

EFFECT ON OTHERS: ____________________

INFLUENCES ON ME: ____________________

I LEARNED: ____________________

RISK: ______________________________

EFFECT ON ME: ______________________________

EFFECT ON OTHERS: ______________________________

INFLUENCES ON ME: ______________________________

I LEARNED: ______________________________

RISK:

EFFECT ON ME:

EFFECT ON OTHERS:

INFLUENCES ON ME:

I LEARNED:

RISK: ______________________________

EFFECT ON ME: ______________________________

EFFECT ON OTHERS: ______________________________

INFLUENCES ON ME: ______________________________

I LEARNED: ______________________________

Chapter 8

Lucky

On a beautiful summer's day, Barnett Helzberg, Jr., of Kansas City, Mo., was threading his way through crowds on Manhattan's Fifth Avenue when he heard a woman call, "Mr. Buffett." Helzberg turned and there, indeed, was the billionaire from Omaha, the owner of Berkshire Hathaway.

As the holder of four shares of Berkshire Hathaway stock, Helzberg knew from reading the company's annual reports that Buffett measured any company he considered buying according to strict financial criteria. Instantly Helzberg realized that his business would fit Buffett's criteria. Ever since his 60th birthday, Helzberg had been thinking about selling his chain of 164 jewelry stores with an annual revenue of roughly $300 million. And here in New York City, he was just yards away from the perfect buyer.

Helzberg walked over to Warren Buffett, introduced himself, and had a 20-second meeting right there on a mid-Manhattan sidewalk. Not long afterward, Buffett received verification of Helzberg's financial information and bought Helzberg Diamond Shops. Buffett says, "That deal never would have happened if I hadn't been walking down that street. I could have been there 30 seconds earlier or 30 seconds later and I never would have met him."

Barnett Helzberg was prepared with facts and figures when he took advantage of an opportunity to talk to Warren Buffett. He was also extraordinarily lucky. Later Heltzberg generously shared his good fortune with many of his employees. Warren Buffett has his own personal story about luck: When he was 20, the Harvard Business School refused Buffett admission. Even though he was demoralized, Buffett began researching other graduate schools. While leafing through Columbia's catalog, he noticed that two men he admired—Benjamin Graham and David Dodd—taught there and enrolled the following month.

"Probably the luckiest thing that ever happened to me was getting rejected by Harvard," Buffett recalls. If he had attended Harvard, he would not have gotten to know Graham, who became his teacher, mentor, and boss. Graham also served on Geico's board, a connection that caused Buffett to buy into Geico, which is still part of Berkshire Hathaway's insurance holdings.

As I've mentioned before, this chapter on luck ties in with Chapter 10 about enthusiasm, and it is intertwined with the previous chapter about being visionary. People who avoid taking risks slide into a rut or deep comfort zone where they feel so warm and cozy and safe that their creativity slowly dissipates. As their creativity dries up, their zest and passion for life disappear; the only way they can energize their creativity is to take risks. Successful people realize that whenever their creative juices are flowing, luck falls in place. To put it another way, their passion for life creates a positive attitude, and they expect and receive self-generated luck.

Be Prepared for Luck

Luck is any force or circumstance that brings us good fortune. Personally, I define luck as opportunity meeting preparedness. Think about that and you'll realize why I am certain that we each create our own luck. My own "preparedness + opportunity = luck" story goes like this:

I worked my way through college at Langemo's Men's Store in Ontario, Calif., which is southeast of Los Angeles. At the beginning of my senior year, owner Herm Langemo started hinting that I should stay on after graduation. Eventually Herm offered me the opportunity to be a junior partner in his men's clothing store; someday, he said, I would own the business. At that time I was planning on getting married and this store seemed like my own little piece of the rock. Gratefully I began looking forward to living and working in Ontario for the rest of my life.

About the time I was happily settled in married life, several salesmen representing our suppliers began urging me to move on. One of them, Dick Nafh, repeatedly reminded me that I wasn't using my potential in that little store. Dick worked for Jockey (now known as Jockey International) and said I could make much better money as a traveling salesman. By then we had a baby on the way and I was reluctant to change; besides, being a traveling salesman was way outside of my comfort zone. Dick suggested that I at least update my resume and slip it into a stamped envelope. There may come a time, he said, when I would decide I had to do something for myself. Perhaps I would need to make more money or need advancement. Then all I had to do was drop that resume in the mail. Dick assured me that having an updated resume ready to go would give me a sense of security. I took that advice to heart, updated my resume, and sealed it in a stamped envelope. Even so, I was positive that I would never use it because, after all, I was going to work in Langemo's in Ontario forever.

About two and a half days after my first son's birth, I looked within and realized I needed to make more money for my family. Between spending time at the hospital and running the store by myself while my partner attended a convention in Las Vegas, I was dead tired. At lunch time on Saturday, I got the envelope with my resume from my car, addressed it to Jockey, and dropped it in the mailbox in front of the store. Little did I know that Jockey would be running an ad for a salesman in the *Los Angeles Times* the next day. As one of the best brand names in the world, Jockey rarely needed to run help-wanted ads.

Jockey called on Monday and told me that out of the 252 applicants, I was one of 25 or so they wanted to interview. The whole process took three nail-biting weeks and I was selected for the job. At 24, I was their youngest salesman. After six months of training, I received my territory and got to work. In the next 12 months, I sold just under $400,000 worth of merchandise at cost. Remember, these were 1960s dollars, when the average retail sale was $6 to $9 for a dozen briefs and maybe some sportswear. Jockey awarded me a lancer ring, indicating that I was one of their top sellers. Because it usually took six to seven years to reach that sales level, I was very proud to wear that lancer ring and I still wear it to remind myself to be prepared for lucky opportunities.

During my next three years with Jockey, I received some good bonuses and I used this money to open a chain of eight men's clothing stores in San Diego. I owed it all to dropping an envelope in the mailbox at just the right time: opportunity + preparedness = luck.

Adopt a Lucky Attitude

Anticipating luck is important because people who think they are lucky tend to take more risks; this increases their chances of success. Take, for instance, two real estate salespeople, one who feels lucky and another who feels unlucky. In determining her advertising budget, the unlucky salesperson may factor in that she is unlucky and budget less money because real estate is very hard to sell right now. The lucky salesperson may increase his advertising budget because the market has been depressed and he wants to attract buyers and sellers. This sales strategy has worked very well for him in the past, and besides, luck's on his side.

People's attitudes toward luck also affect their decision-making. Psychologist Matthew Smith and research fellow Richard Wiseman of the University of Hertfordshire, and psychology professor Peter Harris of the University of Sussex, studied whether clear-thinking, educated adults believe that luck plays a role in the way their lives unfold. In their research, 100 university students told them that luck affects a wide range of events. Therefore, every time some people make major decisions, they add their personal luck to their decision considerations. This is why anticipating luck is so important to achieving success. Anyone who thinks he is unlucky will take fewer risks and decrease his chances for success, while someone who thinks she is lucky takes risks to increase her chances for success.

By the way, Smith defines luck as how each of us sees the world, rather than how the world treats us. His belief that luck is a way of looking at life is based on a study of another 100 people who labeled themselves as lucky or unlucky. Smith asked them to predict heads or tails for 20 coin flips. After each flip, he told the subjects if they had predicted correctly. Both groups accurately predicted the same number of tosses. The lucky subjects knew how many times they had guessed right; however, the unlucky ones underestimated their success. Smith stated that both groups were demonstrating selective recall. Regardless of whether we are lucky or unlucky, we tend to remember events in a way that reflects our perceived good or bad luck.

Why do we use selective recall? Sometimes selective recall helps us keep our self-esteem intact. For instance, while I was the sales manager at two or three companies I frequently ran contests for my salespeople. The winners got a dinner for two or a weekend in a desert condo. At one company, I always knew who would win: Sam. You wouldn't believe how often this salesman won. His co-workers were always saying, "Sam's the luckiest guy; just look at how much luck this guy has. We don't have a chance to win." The ones who said that never came close to winning; but even when he didn't win, Sam was always close because he knew how to work for what he wanted. For Sam—and for the rest of us most of the time—opportunity meeting preparedness causes luck.

Again, the bottom line is that believing makes it so; whether we perceive ourselves as lucky or unlucky governs our actions. A lucky person in a dead-end job would be looking around and networking to find a better job. An unlucky person would see the job as part of a life pattern and stay put.

Rob Hunter, a clinical psychologist who counsels addicted gamblers, points out the importance of learning from both good and bad luck. Say, for example, you hate schmoozing, but you go on a trip to the zoo sponsored by your company and meet a potential spouse. Or perhaps the elephant sprays water on you, causing everyone to laugh except a potential client who compliments your grace under pressure and mentions setting up a business lunch soon. Or, you may be bored and slink away after 15 minutes. In the first two scenarios, by attending the event you opened yourself to the possibility of good luck. In the last scenario, you closed up and went home where you could sulk about your bad luck.

In the next sections, we'll look at some lucky people and then suggest some actions you can take to improve your preparedness for lucky opportunities.

Lucky People

When asked about luck, Brother David Steindl-Rast, a writer and lecturer, answered:

> Luck is not a word that I think of or use much; *gift* is the word, *opportunity*. However, I don't want to be glib about the term *luck* because I am one of the lucky ones. I can think of many crossroads in my life where it could have gone in the unlucky direction and I'm very grateful it didn't. Luck may not be so important, but it makes life a lot easier.

> On the other hand, what we are really given is not good luck or bad luck; that's only the surface. Underneath we are given opportunity, and every bit of bad luck is also an opportunity to make something out of it. We all know people who have made a lot more of their bad luck than others have made out of their good luck. So what counts is how you deal with your opportunity. I admire all the more people who achieve under what we might call unlucky circumstances. In some parts of the world, people are unbelievably stressed by difficulties. I've met people in this country also who have childhoods that were just so unlucky and stressful; I can't even imagine how I personally would have gone through what they did.

When I read Steindl-Rast's comments about making the most of an opportunity, even if it seems like bad luck, I thought of Lee Trevino and Johnny Barfield, who both started out with some pretty bad luck and turned it around. And James Lovell encountered both good and bad luck on *Apollo 13*.

Lee Trevino

Lee Trevino is known for his remark, "The harder I work, the luckier I get." He grew up in a shack with a dirt floor. Fortunately it was on the fringe of a Dallas country club. At age 8, he and his friends spent their days there hunting for golf balls. Trevino believes he was fortunate to have been born in that shack.

At 18, Trevino was a corporal in the Marines who should have gone to Okinawa for reconnaissance training. As luck would have it, a mistake was made, causing him to pull mess duty and stay on the base, where the golf team just happened to have an opening. For the next 18 months, Trevino played every afternoon. By 1995, the earnings of golf's blue-collar hero exceeded $9 million; and still Trevino kept improving his luck by practicing each day.

Johnny Barfield

The son of an Alabama sharecropper, Johnny Barfield was sure he had no special skills that could lift him out of poverty. In 1947 Barfield was a custodian at the University of Michigan, making $1.75 an hour. One day, while thumbing through a magazine on a break, Barfield found an article about contract cleaning. He recalled, "It suddenly dawned on me, there were lots of people out there willing to pay for something I had become expert at."

With the help of his wife, Betty, Barfield began building Barfield Cleaning Services in 1954. Fifteen years later, when ITT bought his business, Barfield realized he had enough contacts in local auto plants to build a second business. In 1995, Bartech Staffing Services employed 1,500 temporary technical workers and made $63 million annually.

Apollo 13

On their way to the moon, James Lovell and his crew ran into a problem on April 13, 1970. Their flight had to be aborted due to a pressure loss in liquid oxygen in a service module and the failure of fuel cells. Lovell believes luck had nothing to do with his and his crew's safe return: "That was strictly brainpower, hard work, and motivation."

When he considers the timing of the explosion that caused the problems, however, he concedes:

> Luck was with me there. There was a window of only a few hours for that explosion. Had it occurred earlier, we would not have had enough electrical power to go all the way around the moon and get home. If it had happened later, when we were in lunar orbit, we wouldn't have had sufficient fuel to get back.

Each of the following lucky people took advantage of the opportunities good luck brought.

Paul Newman

Actor Paul Newman mentions luck when asked about the longevity of his acting career: "Genetics is luck. Appearance is luck....Being born in the United States [is luck]." When questioned about working with Robert Redford again as he did in *Butch Cassidy and the Sundance Kid* and *The Sting*, Newman replied that they haven't found anything of similarly high quality in 25 years. "We were lucky: We did two almost-perfect films together. And to try to maintain that special quality is pretty tough." Notice how Newman does not shut the door completely on a future project. He admits chances are slim, but who knows, maybe Butch and Sundance will luck out again.

Roy Roberts

Roy Roberts is a General Motors vice president and group executive in charge of sales, service, and marketing in North America. Roberts's $10 billion division sells more than 5 million cars each year. When asked how he achieved his position, Roberts answered: "It probably comes from a lot of hard work, great teamwork, being prepared, and a lot of luck." Roberts admits to working awfully hard to be lucky and receiving help from many people. Looking back, he says, "A lot of people who grew up with me didn't make it all the way," referring to his dirt-poor early years. "There's maybe a sliver of difference between them and myself. A lot of them are dead. A lot of them are in prison. And a lot of them are doing other things in life. So I never shy away from luck." While Roberts was growing up, his parents taught their 10 children that they could do anything they set their minds to do. Such a belief would make one lucky indeed.

Roberts described his work ethic this way:

> When I come to work, I come with a zest and a zeal to make things better. Not to maintain, but to make it better. I also come with a knowledge that I have a responsibility, a fiduciary responsibility to this corporation, and I have an awesome responsibility to my people. And I want to function in such a manner that when I move on, there won't be great debates about whether African-Americans and other people can do these types of jobs. That's important to me.

This progressive statement illustrates how the traits of success intertwine and complement each other.

Vanna White

In the early 1980s, Vanna White was a struggling actress when she auditioned with 200 other women for a job on television. She remembers, "I turned letters and my knees shook." Luck was on her side, and she began flipping letters on the world's most-watched game show, *Wheel of Fortune.*

David Wittig

David Wittig was the former co-head of investment banking at Kidder Peabody, and in 1986 Marty Siegel was trying to woo him to move to Drexel Burnham. While having dinner in Siegel's apartment, Wittig recalls, "Siegel was giving me the big schmooze. He told me to ask him anything I wanted.

"I said, 'Okay, Marty. Dennis Levine is in trouble, and there are rumors that Ivan Boesky is next. You once told me you talked to Ivan Boesky every day. Marty, are you clean?'

"Siegel looked me straight in the eyes and said, 'David, I haven't talked to Ivan Boesky in two years.'

"With that, the phone rang and the housekeeper entered the room. 'Mr. Siegel,' she said, 'Mr. Boesky for you on line one.'"

A few months later, Marty Siegel was indicted on charges related to insider trading; he went to prison, as did Ivan Boesky. Drexel Burnham collapsed. And lucky Wittig later became a managing director at Salomon Brothers and retired as a wealthy man; then he started his second career at Western Resources.

James Watson

Nobel Prize winner and scientist James Watson believes that luck significantly affected his development several times.

> When I was an undergraduate at Chicago, I found a little gem of a book, *What Is Life?*, by the theoretical physicist Erwin Schrödinger, who described the gene as being the essence of life. The discovery of this book changed my focus from ornithology to genetics, a field that became one of the defining issues of this century.
>
> Another stroke of luck came when I was turned down for graduate school at Cal Tech and wound up instead at Indiana University working under a remarkable science faculty that included Nobel laureate Dr. H. J. Muller and Dr. Salvador E. Luria. Luria's encouragement and belief in me gave a tremendous boost to my early interest in genetics.

Improve Your Luck

Whether you believe you are lucky or unlucky, you can improve your luck by taking these six actions:

1. Act Lucky

By acting lucky and having a lucky attitude, you attract opportunities to yourself and learn to accept the possibility of success. When making decisions, ask yourself, "How would a lucky person act?" and behave accordingly.

Say, for example, you are selling your house and every real estate agent you interview suggests changing the trim color from purple to brown. A lucky person would hear a clear message: Repaint the trim to improve the chances of a quick sale. A person with bad luck might think about painting and decide she shouldn't have to do anything to sell the house—eventually someone will like purple trim and if no one makes an offer, it's their problem.

2. Plan and Prepare for Success

To create luck for yourself, look within to plan how you are going to get it and to prepare a place for it in your life—then go after what you want. Olympic athletes do this when they plan to spend years preparing to compete in the games.

A person may dream of restoring a classic car, say, a long gas-guzzler from the 1960s. He realizes he'll need more room to work on the car, which wouldn't fit into his tiny garage. Something has to go—either the car or his garage. A lucky person would start building a larger garage for the classic car. An unlucky person would say, "Just my luck, that old Impala's too long for my garage."

When actor Sharon Stone wanted a role in *Basic Instinct*, she secured a copy of the script, dressed in character, and made a surprise visit to director Paul Verhoeven. By following a plan and being prepared, Stone got a role that changed her career.

3. Make Your Own Breaks

When you can't see any way that things are going to change, look within to think creatively, to visualize what you want and how you are going to get it.

Don tried out for his college basketball team as a walk-on. After he made the team, the coach explained that his role would be to play the first team in practice. Although he understood his role, Don still began visualizing himself as a starter on the team and a go-to guy when things got tough. At every practice, he played with concentration and determination, diving after loose balls, practicing his three-point shots, and getting in the face of every opponent. He became the best free-throw shooter on the team.

When several drunken first-stringers were arrested for breaking into cars, they were cut from the team. Don began starting as the point guard. Because his three-point shots were still a weakness, he always got the ball to better shooters. You don't have to be the best at something, but you do have to be prepared to play and have a good work ethic.

Danielle Kennedy, a motivational speaker, wanted to do business with the company that produced her family's favorite product. Over the next eight months, she asked each of her eight children to write a letter to the company's marketing department head explaining that she introduced them to the product and wanted to be a spokesperson or outside speaker for them.

Kennedy was invited to tour the plant, and by coincidence she had a speaking engagement in the same town that day. The head of marketing came to hear her speak and then hired her to speak at their national sales meeting. Coincidentally, she was scheduled to be in the same city the day of the sales meeting. Kennedy believes that when you visualize something you want, "certain forces come together and help make your dream a reality." She recommends being very specific about visions; for instance, she gave herself a year to land that job.

4. Go for It

You can be subtle and still seize an opportunity. If you don't go for it, your chance of success stays at zero. If you do take a chance, you have a 50-50 chance of success—much better odds. Kennedy believes we help luck along when we know what we want and are ready before the opportunity appears.

Rumor has it that actor Fran Drescher took advantage of having a captive audience. Seated next to a CBS executive on a plane, she successfully pitched the idea for her TV show, *The Nanny*. Drescher prepared for this moment by having carefully worked out the idea for the show. She was ready to give it her best shot.

As mentioned at the beginning of this chapter, Barnett Helzberg could pounce when he saw Warren Buffett on a Fifth Avenue sidewalk because he understood Buffett's criteria for purchasing a company and knew it applied to his company.

5. Persist Until You Are an Overnight Success

Instant fame and fortune are rare—very rare. "Instant" fame and fortune come at the end of a long road paved with hard work. Lucky people have a work ethic that does not quit; they pay their dues.

Singer Sheryl Crow had years of experience when she won the Best New Artist Grammy. Crow began studying music as a child and sang backup for seven years; she also wrote songs that other singers recorded.

Illustrator and author Theodor Geisel sent his manuscript out to almost 30 publishers before selling his first Dr. Seuss book. Since then, millions of children and their parents have bought Dr. Seuss books.

6. Stay Positive and Open to Opportunities.

You can turn adversity into an advantage when you learn to survive rejection. People who believe they are lucky all feel positive about their lives and their luck, even in the midst of chaos. Look within to help you stay positive so you can continue to attract lucky opportunities. Luck is passed on to those who are most receptive, so pay attention to what is going on around you.

A woman we'll call Peggy Sue worked for an accounting firm for 10 years. When she was fired, Peggy Sue was livid and shocked. In reality, she should have been dancing with joy, because she detested her job. When she cooled down, Peggy Sue realized how many contacts she had due to her former job; soon she had started her own accounting firm and was networking furiously. Two years later, she was looking for an assistant. Getting fired wasn't the end of the world, it was the beginning of a new world.

Journal Notes About Being Lucky: Developing the Qualities of Success

Choose one of the six actions that can prepare you for lucky opportunities and write down five ways you can put this action into practice. Perform your five ways for the 21 days. After trying the first action, write about how it helped you improve your luck or how it did not. If it did not, discuss why it was not helpful.

Then choose another action and list five ways you can put it into practice. Put these ways into practice for the next 21 days. For the second action, again write what happened. If it did not help you to improve your luck, discuss why.

After trying two actions to prepare yourself for lucky opportunities, describe how you feel about luck now. Has your belief in luck changed, and if so, how has it changed?

FIRST ACTION TO IMPROVE LUCK: ______________________

FIRST WAY: ______________________

____

SECOND WAY: ______________________

____

THIRD WAY: ______________________

____

FOURTH WAY: ______________________

____

FIFTH WAY: ______________________

____

HOW DID THIS ACTION IMPROVE YOUR LUCK?

____

____

____

HOW WAS IT NOT HELPFUL?

____

____

SECOND ACTION TO IMPROVE LUCK: ____________________

FIRST WAY: ____________________

SECOND WAY: ____________________

THIRD WAY: ____________________

FOURTH WAY: ____________________

FIFTH WAY: ____________________

HOW DID THIS ACTION IMPROVE YOUR LUCK?

HOW WAS IT NOT HELPFUL?

HOW DO YOU FEEL ABOUT LUCK?

HOW HAS YOUR BELIEF IN LUCK CHANGED?

Chapter 9

Excels

Last year, when I was conducting a training session at Nordstrom, I stopped in the men's room for associates. After closing the door, I looked around and almost backed out, thinking I was in the ladies' room. Looking around again, I realized that I was in the right room, but this men's room was like none I had ever seen.

Framed paintings hung on the freshly painted walls. Bottles of cologne stood on a tray close to a stack of fluffy hand towels. A bouquet of fresh flowers graced the other end of the counter; they were reflected in a tall mirror running the length of the counter. The air smelled fresh and every bit of chrome sparkled.

And then I saw it—a simple card tent folded to stand beneath the bouquet. Addressed to Nordstrom associates, it expressed appreciation for their efforts to provide excellent service. The writer of the card, a division manager, thanked the associates for providing memorable shopping experiences for Nordstrom customers.

Nordstrom pulls out all the stops in its effort to make shopping an extraordinary experience for customers. Its management excels at empowering associates to do their best work because each associate who excels helps Nordstrom provide excellent service.

If you want to be successful, develop an appreciation for excelling in your work, your family, your social circle, and your community. Excelling is not a matter of being picky or too critical. Excelling is the ability to see the possibility of improvement instead of continuing the ordinary-same-old.

Pursue Excellence

This quote from Vince Lombardi, legendary coach of the Green Bay Packers, is one of my favorites: "As far as excellence is concerned, we can never be perfect, but in our striving for perfection, we will achieve excellence." Note that Lombardi emphasizes the possible (striving) and not the impossible (achieving perfection). A person who excels can make incremental improvements in the quality of a product, service, or relationship. On a personal level, pursuing excellence means you are willing to look within to review your relationships and see how you can create first-class connections with friends, co-workers, your family, and community members. The process of excelling is an all-out effort to do the absolute, no-holds-barred best that you can.

As any junkyard full of old cars documents, excellence cannot be a static quality; it has a short shelf life because the bar can always be raised, the product or relationship always improved. For example, when people began wearing glasses, they thought having corrected 20/20 vision was truly excellent until they heard about contact lenses that improved sight without glasses. Today, laser surgery gives people who require it extra sharp 20/10 vision without glasses or contacts. The bar has been raised again.

When you look within, find out what motivates you to achieve excellence. Why do you want to excel at something? And how can you go about doing that? There are four qualities you can develop to motivate yourself and to support others as they strive to achieve excellence. According to Aristotle, truth, goodness, beauty, and unity are qualities that create a foundation for excellence. Next we look at how to develop these four qualities on an individual level and on a business level, then we demonstrate how business organizations nurture these qualities as they continually strive for excellence.

Making Excellence a Personal Value

Before attempting to create a desire for excellence in others, we need to learn how truth, goodness, beauty, and unity can create a foundation for excellence within ourselves.

Truth

To achieve excellence in our own lives, we must make telling the truth a priority. This means allowing no wiggle room when you are talking with your spouse or children or in-laws or friends. Telling the flat-out truth isn't the most popular virtue around, but mix it with kindness and give it a trial. At first you may have a problem because you are used to being polite and saying what people want to hear. Can you risk telling your spouse the truth? I should hope so, because this frees up your spouse to do the same. No successful marriage can be based on half-truths or lies.

Your children may not always like the truth, but they'll respect you for telling it. It's the same for your relatives and in-laws; many families have subjects they do not talk about, usually because these subjects are painful. Putting up invisible fences around certain subjects, such as Uncle Mike who's serving a life sentence in jail, doesn't solve any problems; it just drives the pain deeper. Not talking about problems doesn't teach youngsters how to deal with life; the truth helps children learn to face life realistically.

Goodness

Henry David Thoreau wrote, "There is never an instant's truce between virtue and vice. Goodness is the only investment that never fails." Goodness is looking within and doing what your heart says is right. Goodness is what makes you a trustworthy and loyal friend, and sometimes goodness means you do what's right rather than what's popular. It's treating people the way you want to be treated. Truth and goodness are so closely related, I don't think you can have one without the other.

Goodness implies being able to get over resentment caused by disappointment and rejection. Goodness also implies being able to accept other people's peculiarities. There wouldn't be so much road rage if we let the jackasses be jackasses. Yelling "Why don't you look where you're going?" may make us feel better, but doesn't stop the jerks who cut us off from cutting others off. Remember that each of us has the ability to control only ourselves and our responses to people and events in our lives. We cannot control other people or their actions. All that we control is ourselves and our responses—and when you think about it, that's a pretty good arrangement.

Beauty

Have you ever noticed how much better you feel when driving a clean car? Being able to see through the windshield and not seeing stains on the floor mats makes a big difference. That feeling is why all of your surroundings should be pleasing; beauty rests and refreshes your soul because beauty begins in the soul.

Have you ever met people who are not at first glance outstandingly attractive, but as you got to know them, they became beautiful? That's soul coming through from within. I saw an example of this when visiting an ill child for Make-A-Wish. My partner and I stopped to see a boy I'll call Jorge. At first, we were amazed that a family with eight children could survive with only two bedrooms. But despite its size, the apartment was almost spotless, as were the children.

Our amazement turned to admiration of the children's gracious manners and obvious love for one another. When I gave each child a small wrapped present, each child thanked me and held the gift until receiving permission to open it. Jorge's tidy home was one of the most beautiful homes I have ever visited; it stays in my soul and warms my heart.

Similar to a home situation, contributing to beauty at work can be as simple as cleaning up your own stuff by putting away anything that you are not using. Despite a few weak claims by people who haven't seen the tops of their desks for years, they do not work better when surrounded by clutter. Researchers have documented that our environment has a major impact on us. A messy environment creates slovenly thinking and poor-quality work; furthermore, cluttered surroundings impact the way we carry ourselves and the way we talk to people.

As a manager, I always set an example by keeping my office and desk clean and organized. I reminded my employees that even when they were talking on the phone to customers, they should have their desks tidy, their information organized, and smiles on their faces. A cluttered desk is distracting because it confuses your mind. When surrounded by a mess, you can't think as clearly or speak as concisely and to the point.

You also can reflect beauty in your appearance. You've probably noticed that in some offices on casual Fridays, workers look like they just finished cleaning their basements. If you value beauty, look as wrinkle-free as the weather permits. Try for a crisp appearance when you dress for casual Fridays; it will cheer up everyone around you.

Unity

Unity means that you are the same in each of your roles. Working for unity also is important when you are part of a group—family, work, community, church, and so on. To be effective, groups must be unified, otherwise they spend their time infighting. Examples: Astronauts flying around in space are effective groups that must work together to survive. Members of the U.S. Congress, on the other hand, feel no compulsion to work together.

John Elway

Recent NFL retiree John Elway appears to have committed himself to success; he certainly demonstrates the qualities of excellence. For instance, Elway demonstrates goodness. He's been dubbed "the saint of Denver" for his patience and willingness to meet fans. Elway has been stopped in theaters, restaurants, and freeway off-ramps by fans wanting autographs. This is a good example of virtue being its own reward. His popularity has allowed Elway to make millions of dollars in endorsements.

According to Dean Bonham, who is in sports and entertainment marketing, "Everyone I have spoken with about his business acumen says quite simply he is one of the more knowledgeable, thoughtful, strategic businessmen in professional sports today." With several partners, Elway created a very successful chain of car dealerships that they sold in 1997. Although car salespeople are not known for their honesty, Elway may have been an exception.

David Treadwell, a lawyer and former Broncos kicker, sums up Elway the man with this: "I don't think there's any question that John's been a tremendous asset to the community of Denver, as a player and off the field as a community leader, not just as a businessman." Obviously, Elway is a team player who understands unity and the beauty of working together.

Creating Excellence in the Business World

Too often in modern workplaces, excellence and worker satisfaction do not coexist. Even though disgruntled workers achieve what management calls excellence, they feel stressed and pressured. By incorporating truth, goodness, beauty, and unity into their business environments, firms can help their employees feel good about what they are doing and sustain the excellence they want to achieve.

Truth

Human beings need truth just as they need food, air, and water. Instead, they may find themselves hesitating to tell the truth about problems at work or being intimidated by organizational politics. This is one of the toughest things in the corporate world—telling the truth to your employees and sharing truth with your associates. I have found that as I moved up the corporate ladder in some companies, employees tended not to tell the whole truth because by reserving some facts they could retain control over their areas. In some firms (though certainly not all) job stability comes from telling half-truths, or not telling the truth at all.

The perfect solution to this lack of corporate truthfulness is the Servant Leadership program, which has become a buzzword in corporate America. Servant Leadership teaches that leaders have to practice the abilities and traits of a servant. Although many have written about this form of leadership, my favorite is Mark Maier, Ph.D., whom I've heard speak several times. Maier is the founding chair of the Organizational Leadership program at Chapman University, and in 1999 he received a Distinguished Educator Award.

Dr. Maier has spent years researching one of the greatest failures in NASA history, the explosion of the *Challenger* during its seventh flight in January of 1986. Maier has concluded that seven lives were lost due primarily to the withholding of truth and secondarily to the telling of half-truths and the overlooking of facts that were true. The people involved wanted to make sure that their departments looked good. Maier found there was no good reason for the *Challenger* to explode 73 seconds after liftoff. It all came down to not telling or withholding the truth when questions were asked.

Telling the truth with kindness enhances the workplace; uncaring, unfeeling truth-telling destroys it. Tom Morris, who wrote a book about Aristotle and business success, believes sharing "truth in the right way multiplies truth and strengthens the organization."

For instance, many times while urging employees to do more work to improve the company's bottom line, companies refuse to tell their employees exactly how much money they made last year or how well they are doing this year. Thus, employees have no incentive because the true situation has been withheld from them. They are good enough to do the work, but not important enough to be trusted with bottom-line figures.

Goodness

Goodness creates an atmosphere of trust and loyalty between a business and its suppliers and between the firm and its employees. Obviously, goodness must permeate a firm's business ethics. Organizations that practice goodness treat their employees with kindness, respect, and fairness; their employees return the favor by working to create a stronger firm. Pacific Life Insurance is such a company. One of the world's larger life insurance firms, Pacific Life has very low turnover and extremely high employee loyalty because of the way the firm treats their employees. This company believes in training their employees and treating them with respect. I know that firsthand because I've done a lot of work with Pacific Life.

Beauty

Workplaces can have several types of beauty; the most obvious occurs when management beautifies the actual place where people work. People who work in pleasant surroundings perform at higher levels because they feel good about their workplace. Other types of beauty at work include empowering people to solve business problems and delighting an associate or customer through good work. Employees who find beauty in their work naturally derive greater satisfaction from it.

Unity

Everyone yearns to be part of something greater than himself; nowhere is this more evident than at work. The unity and connectedness that employees feel at work fulfills deep psychological and spiritual needs. People need to do more than simply make money; they need to make a difference. And the company needs their contributions because taken together all of the people in a company are smarter than any single individual. Author Warren Bennis points out that "We love to problem solve. It's the task we evolved for. We especially love to do it in partnership with others whom we respect." The following story about the Manhattan Project illustrates the importance of unity in the workplace.

The Manhattan Project

Technicians came to Los Alamos, N.M., from all over the United States to work on the Manhattan Project, a crash project to produce an atomic bomb during World War II. Although they did energy calculations on primitive computers, the techs knew nothing about what their calculations meant or the whole project. They processed numbers one after another slowly and badly until Richard Feynman asked his superiors to tell the techs how important their work was. J. Robert Oppenheimer, later known as the father of the atomic bomb, explained to the techs how instrumental their work was in making the Manhattan Project a success.

Once the techs understood the importance of their jobs, they worked nearly 10 times faster. They also found new, better ways of doing the work; they invented new programs and worked through the night.

Excelling in the Workplace

The following organizations differ in just about every way possible, except for one: they all are aiming for excellence and they train their employees to excel. As a result, their employees demonstrate the qualities of truth, goodness, beauty, and unity.

Walt Disney World

All the world's a stage, especially when you're in the Magic Kingdom. Walt Disney World has embraced Performance Excellence, a program to make employees active partners in the company's success and to increase customer loyalty and satisfaction. This program started in 1993; five years later the guest return rate had increased 10 percent and employee turnover rates had dropped.

To enhance their performance excellence, during training Disney employees experience firsthand how guests feel when treated badly and when treated well. For example, during training while a manager was describing the upscale restaurant's operation, a new dishwasher noticed a glass with lipstick stains, fine china dishes with crusts of food on the rims, and spotted silverware. When a manager asked why she looked distracted, she explained that the dishes were dirty. "Imagine," said the manager, "that you are a guest who will spend $100 for that meal." The manager purposely gave the new dishwasher an opportunity to speak out about the dirty dishes, so she would learn that Disney employees are expected to tell the truth about problems.

Such training enables employees to take responsibility for their guests' treatment, and sometimes to provide the beauty of a delightful experience. One example: A custodian was sweeping up after a Magic Kingdom parade when a guest asked where to find a cup of ice. The custodian couldn't leave his large vacuum cleaner unattended so he pointed to a drink cart across the street. Then, he radioed the guest's request to the drink cart operator. When the guest walked up, the cart operator handed him a cup filled with ice saying, "I believe you're looking for a cup of ice." The guest was amazed and probably still tells this great service story.

Employees at Disney World soon learn that whether they are sweeping streets or washing dishes, their job is to create happiness. Disney employees are encouraged to connect emotionally with guests; this improves the staff's level of creativity when serving them. Staff members also are expected to take responsibility. In Disney's upscale restaurants, the wait staff have been empowered to refund guests' checks without management approval.

If employees see a problem, they are to solve it. For example, when housekeepers at the Wilderness Lodge noticed that their runners were spending several hours delivering extra pillows each day, they began keeping track of the exact time involved. Then they brainstormed to improve the situation. Their simple solution—placing two extra pillows in the closets—reduced the hours per day to minutes per week. In seven days the lodge recovered the cost of 1,500 pillows.

Walt Disney World's Performance Excellence program empowers workers to work together to find solutions, to be truthful, to create beauty through the park's appearance and their treatment of guests, and to feel good about their jobs.

Nordstrom

As mentioned earlier in this chapter, Nordstrom offers extraordinary customer service and selection. Since 1901, its motto has been: "Offer an exceptional selection of quality merchandise, always at a value. Service the customer's needs first and strive to make every shopping experience a good one." Standing behind this motto, Nordstrom supports each employee's entrepreneurial spirit: Individual buyers select merchandise that they know their customers will like and regional managers decide where to build new stores. The Seattle-based retail chain's only instruction to its sales associates is "Use your good judgment in all situations."

By empowering its staff and managers to do their very best, this retail giant allows them to be truthful (as in, "We don't carry that brand, but Marshall Field's does") and frees up their goodness (as in, "Would you like me to call Marshall Field's for you?"). Nordstrom stores reflect beauty, and their staff and managers, unity. As mentioned in the opening story, I've enjoyed working with Nordstrom many times.

Ritz-Carlton Hotel Company

When people pay a premium for hotel excellence, the hotel had better surpass their service expectations. The Ritz-Carlton almost always does. At its 35 hotels around the world, this company must ensure that employees understand their jobs and can think on their feet. To this end, the human resources department begins by using psychological tests to carefully screen applicants. Such testing can indicate if a person who wants to be a housekeeper pays attention to detail, or if a prospective doorman is a people person. Only one out of every 10 applicants is hired.

Ritz-Carlton creates a caring, supportive, and energizing environment for its new employees. New hires receive 120 hours of customer service training; each works with a trainer who explains individual tasks, supervises the new hire's learning, and reviews performance. In addition to technical training, new employees learn how to instantly pacify guests; they can do this because they are empowered to resolve guests' problems. For example, a waiter who hears a guest complaining about a bad TV will report it to the engineering department and later call the guest to make sure the problem was resolved.

All employees begin their shifts with a daily 10- or 15-minute meeting. Here discussions may address why the Ritz-Carlton is in business and its commitment to great customer service, or they may recognize and celebrate staff members to create a sense of belonging. Ritz-Carlton also surveys its employees to determine how the company can serve them. The company's philosophy is that if employees' needs are not met, customers' needs won't be met. If you are wondering where you heard that attitude before, see Chapter 2.

By empowering employees to solve problems, Ritz-Carlton allows their truth and goodness to shine. The beauty of the hotels is matched by the staff's professional treatment of guests. Through extensive training and daily meetings, employees are proud to be part of a leader in the hospitality industry.

Manugistics

Since 1986, this software company has been guided by a value system called the Elements of Excellence. Manugistics CEO William Gibson believed that the company's success depended on its values being tied to its business strategy. When he asked clients and his staff to brainstorm a value system, they came up with three Elements of Excellence. Coincidentally, the elements reflect goodness, beauty, unity, and truth:

1. We treat others as we would like to be treated. (Goodness and beauty)
2. Partnership with our clients results in superior products. (Unity)
3. Team success is more important than personal glory. (Unity and truth)

Manugistics walks its talk: It put the first element into practice by reassuring the employees of an acquired company, Rover, that they still had jobs. Rover's former CEO is now a high-level executive at Manugistics. Not many CEOs of acquired companies can make that statement. With each acquisition, the company continues to sell itself to the employees it acquires.

The second element of excellence was obvious when a large Canadian company insisted that Manugistics' human relations people do a presentation for them as part of a purchasing process. The Canadians liked what they saw; the people aspect attracted them to Manugistics. Also, companies in partnership with Manugistics appreciate the give-and-take relationship between staffs.

The third element is visible in Manugistics's teamwork environment. The company's turnover is lower than the industry standard. The head of human resources, Carl DiPietro, says, "Empowerment is an important concept here because it's absolutely mandatory that we rely on these good people that we hired to make decisions and move us forward."

Journal Notes About Excellence: Developing the Qualities of Success

Next to each of the four qualities of excellence, write one action you can take to emphasize that quality in your life. Be specific about the action you intend to take, such as, "I'm going to increase the beauty of our home by putting things away and getting rid of things we don't need and never use." Then take appropriate action within the next three weeks.

Write about how the four actions you chose to increase excellence in your life have worked out. Can you see a difference in how you act or react? For each quality, add two more actions that you can take to excel.

TRUTH: ____________________

WHAT WORKED AND WHAT DID NOT: ____________________

TWO ADDITIONAL ACTIONS I CAN TAKE TO INCREASE TRUTH:

Goodness:

What Worked And What Did Not:

Two Additional Actions I Can Take To Increase Goodness:

BEAUTY:

WHAT WORKED AND WHAT DID NOT:

TWO ADDITIONAL ACTIONS I CAN TAKE TO INCREASE BEAUTY:

UNITY:

WHAT WORKED AND WHAT DID NOT:

TWO ADDITIONAL ACTIONS I CAN TAKE TO INCREASE UNITY:

RESULTS OF THE FOUR ACTIONS AFTER THREE WEEKS:

Chapter 10

Enthusiastic

Tourists are absolutely flocking to watch Seattle's flying fish. Once you are downtown, just head for the bay and look for historic Pike Place Market, then follow the crowds inside to the World Famous Pike Place Fish Market. Not many businesses can boast of drawing visitors from all over the world to watch fish flying through the air, tossed by busy employees who enjoy their jobs. Each time I've been there, World Famous has been packed.

Despite employees' antics, World Famous takes seafood very seriously. The market bases its reputation for selling only the finest, freshest seafood on its commitment to superior customer service. The staff has more than 125 years of experience in the seafood industry, and employee retention and training are company values just as important as having fun.

I learned about World Famous on my favorite training video, "Fish," which features a World Famous employee of 18 years who describes his job this way: "It takes enthusiasm, and I've got it!" A close-up of his face lights up the whole screen.

I've been looking forward to writing this chapter because every time I stand in front of an audience, one of my goals is to create enthusiasm. Of course, I'm there to impart information too, but I know that listeners lacking enthusiasm for their lives or jobs won't act on this information. Or, as I mentioned in the Preface, maybe they aren't ready for my message; they may hear what I say, but aren't really listening to me or looking within.

I believe in the importance of enthusiasm because I've seen so many enthusiastic people become successful, while those lacking enthusiasm go nowhere and are miserable. This chapter begins with a definition of enthusiasm, briefly looks at researchers' conclusions about enthusiasm, gives characteristics of enthusiastic people, describes actions you can take to develop your enthusiasm, and explains how you can use enthusiasm to encourage your employees.

Live Life With Enthusiasm

Writer Herb Ashley defines enthusiasm as "the ingredient that provides the spark in life...the extinguisher of mental agony brought on by fear, suspicion, and doubt of others and of self. Because it defines self-acceptance, self-awareness, and self-discipline, it helps people become themselves without having to apologize to anybody, thereby generating a personal harmony with oneself." Although enthusiasm springs from deep within us, it is not just about self. It is also about all those with whom we interact. Ashley adds, "Lastly, enthusiasm encourages individuals to aim high and aim again if they miss."

Enthusiasm Really Rocks

Enthusiastic people always see a broader picture full of opportunity and intriguing possibilities; they see so much more than those lacking enthusiasm, who see only the same old same old. That's why enthusiasm shakes things up. Enthusiasm really does rock.

Researchers have found that enthusiastic people have greater peace of mind, higher self-esteem, a stronger sense of well-being, better physical health, and increased success in school and at work. According to psychiatrist Harold Bloomfield, M.D., "People who have a positive mental outlook have a distinct edge in life over others who are less enthusiastic."

A professor of psychology at the University of Kansas, C. R. Snyder, Ph.D., found that college freshmen who thought they would perform well in their classes actually did; those lacking enthusiastic outlooks scored lower. Likewise, women on diets who remained enthusiastic were quicker to lose weight than those with a less positive outlook.

A study at the University of Michigan found that pessimistic students were ill twice as many days as optimistic students; they also visited the doctor four times as often as optimistic students.

These studies back up a centuries-old statement from the Talmud: "We see things as we are, not as they are." Thus, if we look within so that we can approach each day with enthusiasm—whether it is natural or developed—even difficulties appear to have positive sides. This reminds me of the change in Sammy Sosa, who reportedly was known as a moody, selfish player in 1998 when he was busy trying to prove himself to everyone. Even so, he was voted the Most Valuable Player that year.

In 1999, however, Sosa became playful with his public and his teammates. He explains the change this way:

> It was hard for me...because nobody understood where I was coming from. Now everybody cheers and gives me the respect I need and the love I need. That's why my whole game has changed, because I feel loved. I come to my dugout, hang out with my teammates, and be friends with everybody. That's something that has helped me a lot.

Sosa's change of attitude began in the off-season, when he appeared frequently at functions and raised money for his homeland, the Dominican Republic, which was still suffering from the aftereffects of a hurricane.

During a spring game, Sosa was hit on the head by a baseball thrown from the stands by a mother seeking an autograph for her son. "I should sue you," Sosa said to her, signing with a big smile. Ever since Sosa realized that he was loved, he has reacted with love and enthusiasm for life and others.

Learned Behavior

Some researchers believe enthusiasm is learned behavior that parents either encourage or discourage during childhood. Auke Tellegen, Ph.D., a professor of psychology at the University of Minnesota, points out that "Some people seem to be born with a lot of joy juice," due to higher levels of the brain chemical dopamine. He cites research on identical twins who were raised in different families: Typically, they share the same level of enthusiasm. Does this mean that if you don't inherit joy juice, enthusiasm is unattainable? Not really. Whether we inherit enthusiasm or work to acquire it, we can use enthusiasm to improve our own lives and those of others. It's all a matter of looking within and spreading the enthusiasm we find or develop.

In this life we control two important things: our attitudes and our effort. These are the very roots of enthusiasm. When we are enthusiastic about something, we display a positive attitude and show that we care. That's why enthusiasm is part of luck; this is another time when the traits mentioned in this book complement each other. It's a fact: Lucky people are enthusiastic and enthusiastic people are lucky.

Enthusiasm Is Catching

Enthusiasm is contagious; you can't give it if you don't have it, and you can't catch it if you are not around it. So seek out people with enthusiasm and hang with them until you catch it and pass it on to the next person. If all of you do this, our country could have a badly needed epidemic of enthusiasm.

Subway rider and author Marc Myers tells about a New York City subway train that shuttles between Times Square and Grand Central Terminal. After riders get off in Times Square, it takes a minute or two for passengers to board the train. Myers noticed that sometimes the wait was slightly longer because a new conductor waited for people jogging to catch the train. At other times, he closed the doors and departed on time, much to the chagrin of people strolling toward the train. Ever curious, Myers asked the conductor why he sometimes waited and other times closed the doors.

"If people are tryin', I'm buyin'," the conductor said. "I like helping people who make an effort to get on. I'll hold the door a few extra seconds for them. But if catching this train doesn't matter to you, it sure doesn't matter to me. You can take the next one."

As the conductor's actions pointed out, enthusiasm is definitely contagious. We may not understand enthusiastic people at first, but we enjoy helping and just being around them.

Another example from Myers is a cigar seller named Jam on the island of St. Bart's in the Caribbean. Coming from a poor background in Tunisia, Jam says:

> I am excited to be living such a comfortable life now. I have a great wife and kids, and I love them very much. I love people. I enjoy their happiness and share mine with them. When I'm excited, they become more excited. They may come in serious or reserved because they don't know me, but they

always leave in a better mood. I also love seeing how my personality rubs off on them. Sometimes my spirit makes them withdraw, but once they've been here for a few times, they realize this is how I really am.

Enthusiasm is catching. At first, you're afraid when someone is happy because you think the person is trying to get you to drop your guard so they can steal from you. But when you see the enthusiastic person doesn't want anything, you become enthusiastic, too. Enthusiasm is also good for business, but only because it makes doing business fun. Enthusiasm makes people excited and makes them feel special. There are other places to buy cigars on this island—and all over the Caribbean. There are larger stores. But there is no other store where you're going to find me. Do people buy more cigars because of it? I don't know, but, I'm sure they do. But I do know that they're here for more than the cigars. They call months later to see how I'm doing, they send me gifts when they get home, they're just happy to have met me and I'm happy to have met them. Enthusiasm brings people to you—and people bring luck.

Enthusiastic people like Jam do four things that help others catch their enthusiasm:

1. Smile because a smile is an ice breaker. They smile because they are warm and inviting people. They smile because a genuine smile that bubbles up from within is something people remember. They smile because a smile puts people on both sides at ease. If enthusiasm is not a natural response for you, practice genuine smiles in front of a mirror and then consciously smile more for the next three weeks. Why don't you put a smile on your face right this moment? No one's watching, why not enjoy it?

2. Look into the other person's eyes during a conversation. Enthusiastic people do this to really focus on what the other person is saying, instead of staring elsewhere and planning what to say next. If you decide to give smiling more of a try, follow that up by really looking people in the eye when you speak to them. This makes unenthusiastic people very uneasy, so adjust to each situation while showing enthusiasm.

3. Use enthusiasm naturally, so that it is appropriate to the occasion and people with whom they are interacting. For instance, a funeral director would exhibit low-key enthusiasm in deference to grieving families; while a soccer coach should be much more enthusiastic. At a charity fund-raiser, positive people can be quite a bit more enthusiastic. Think chameleon and match your enthusiasm to the occasion.
4. Are more enthusiastic about others than themselves. Enthusiastic people look for and praise the best in others; for themselves, they reserve a bit of an aw-shucks-it-was-just-luck humility. Such an approach is very effective because it shows that enthusiasm is not self-centered but centered on the results of other people's efforts, and how that effort has affected others. Enthused people see beyond their own actions; for instance, they may comment on their luck in winning an award and point out that they received a lot of help from other members of a team or firm.

Enthusiasm Is a Life Tool

A veteran salesman once suggested to young salespeople: "Make your calls when you're up. Much of your effectiveness lies in your own mind. If you're feeling on top, it's contagious and you infect the buyer with that same enthusiasm." This advice works on all levels of life because all of us consistently are selling our beliefs and concerns to family, friends, neighbors, government officials, and business associates. This brings up two points:

1. First, all of us are more enthused sometimes than others, so keep in touch with your natural mood swings. Even though our moods change, generally we can maintain an enthusiastic outlook about life and fake it to survive a few really bad mood days. As enthusiasm becomes engrained in our psyches, we have fewer bad days.
2. Second, when you are feeling good and enthusiastic is the most effective time to impart lessons: Parents can sell values and lifestyle choices enthusiastically to children, or employees can talk to the boss about a raise.

Six Steps to Develop Your Enthusiasm

Life isn't fair. Not everyone is born with enthusiasm, and some have their enthusiasm stifled at an early age. Anyone can look within, however, and decide to take these six simple steps to create a more enthusiastic personality:

1. Counter negative thinking by developing a more positive outlook on your life. When you arrive home, do you groan when you notice the grass is taller than your oldest child and the shrubs tower over you like trees, not to mention that your children will need all of your attention tonight because your spouse is going to be late, and on and on.... Or, do you notice a comfortable home in good repair with your healthy children racing down the walk to greet you?

2. Start doing activities you enjoy; stop waiting for someday when you have time. Make a list of these activities and do one a week. According to author Erik Olesen, studies have found that "people who do more of what they enjoy rate their lives better within six months."

3. Hang out with enthusiastic people. If your friends are bitter, cynical people, they can't help you be more upbeat and positive because they haven't a clue about enthusiasm. Remember, if you want to soar like an eagle, then don't hang out with ducks—and there are lots of ducks.

4. Get inspired. Read a classic, watch a classic, or listen to classical music that helps you feel better about yourself and the world in general. (But save all the tear-jerkers and blues songs until you can truthfully say, "I am enthusiastic about life.") Become a classic by doing some work for Make-A-Wish, working to prevent child abuse, or going for whatever you value.

5. Take on a new challenge instead of giving an excuse about why you can't do it. Learning something new or doing a challenging activity creates enthusiasm that spreads to other things you do. Such an activity doesn't have to be rappelling down the tallest building in town; it can be taking a home landscaping course or fencing lessons or cooking lessons.

6. Remind yourself to be enthusiastic and upbeat. Visualize an enthusiastic occurrence in your life and remember how you felt. Take time to savor that feeling and to remember similar times when you were enthusiastic. Such memories prove that if you were upbeat once, you can be again.

Enthusiastic Entrepreneurs

Scratch an entrepreneur and usually you will find someone wildly enthusiastic about an idea and totally convinced of its success. An entrepreneur with a new unproven idea actually expects to change the industry or the world or how people live. Entrepreneurs put into practice essayist Ralph Waldo Emerson's statement: "Nothing great was ever achieved without enthusiasm."

Professor Ian C. MacMillan of the Wharton School at the University of Pennsylvania has counseled thousands of start-up wannabes. He found that entrepreneurs see their product or company in their mind's eye; this vision is so clear that they believe they know exactly what they need to do to be successful. And sometimes they're right. For example:

- Ken Olsen knew how to make computers less expensively than IBM. He started Digital Equipment Corp.
- Merritt Sher of San Francisco noticed that although small specialty stores were often overshadowed by large department stores in suburban malls, they could survive in smaller strip malls. He explained his vision like this: "You suddenly understand how everything fits together. And then you want to demonstrate that you have the understanding."
- Robert DeNiro knew how to turn the Brooklyn Naval Yard into a successful East Coast movie studio. In true entrepreneurial fashion, actor DeNiro commented, "I could be wrong a little bit here and there, but you cannot fail at this."
- Arthur Pappas, who started a biotech venture capital firm near Research Triangle Park, N.C., leaves the early technical and financial details of business proposals to others. He prefers to focus on the character and commitment of the management team members of firms seeking capital. He believes

the "people with vision or insight see something and are driven to its endpoint. You can hear it in their voices."

- Bill McGowan, founder of MCI, worked for 10 years to end AT&T's monopoly of long-distance service. When people say to him, "Ten years! How could you do that?" McGowan responds, "Do you mean you think it was stupid? I never thought it would take that long. I thought I could do it overnight."

This brief sampling of entrepreneurs shows that they need all the enthusiasm and commitment they can muster, not to mention a good dose of luck.

Creating Enthusiasm

After getting a business up and running, an entrepreneur must keep the enthusiasm flowing by giving employees positive feedback about their work. Ken Blanchard and Sheldon Bowles, authors of *Gung Ho*, suggest that you try to catch your employees in the act of doing something right. (This works well with children, too.) Blanchard and Bowles point out that all businesses need employees with boundless enthusiasm, energy, and dedication to their jobs.

Employers such as Nordstrom, Disney, Ritz-Carlton, and Wal-Mart put a lot of effort into employee relations. They do their best to treat their employees with care and respect, and to increase energy and enthusiasm in their companies. Blanchard and Bowles have some suggestions about providing employee feedback that can stimulate enthusiasm. In essence, you must catch your people doing something right and then cheer them on.

- Be immediate with your congratulations for employees. Don't wait a week or a month; cheer them on immediately.
- Tell your employees how their work makes you feel; tell them what a great job they are doing.
- Show employees that you know they can handle a job by giving it to them and letting them run with it without interfering.
- Instead of having an employee of the month, have many employees of the moment, who can be cheered on immediately.

- ➢ Use your unlimited supply of congratulations; cash bonuses are always appreciated, but most companies have limited funds available. A manager has an unlimited supply of enthusiastic congratulations available.

John Adams of Adams and Adams Building Services, a janitorial service, believes in showing employees that they are valued. To carry out Adams' Instantaneous Recognition and Awards Program, managers carry congratulatory note cards to reward any employee on the spot for a job well done. As well as the note card, employees receive two tickets to fill out for a biannual drawing for prizes such as VCRs and vacations.

To end this chapter about enthusiasm, I have another story. Recently I read a line that really stuck with me: Storytellers rule the world! It made me realize just how powerful we storytellers are because people pay more attention to stories told with enthusiasm than to preaching or teaching. For example, I believe premier storyteller Ronald Reagan was the first president to invite exemplary people to take a bow at his State of the Union address. During his speech, Reagan told their stories and lead the applause; these human interest stories told Americans about the real state of our union. Since then, most presidents have continued this tradition of telling the stories of extraordinary citizens who honor us by their efforts.

The following is one of Zig Ziglar's hundreds of stories. It sums up how much of a difference enthusiasm can make:

> Railroad employees were standing around a truck that sold snacks and drinks, taking a coffee and burrito break when a limousine pulled up and a well-dressed man stepped out. Heading for the truck, he bought something and then walked over to one worker and offered his hand, saying, "Hello Travis, how are you doing?"
>
> Travis dropped his cigarette and shook hands, answering, "I'm doing fine, just fine, Jim. See you still like those little fruit pies."
>
> With a chuckle, Jim answered, "Trav, I'm addicted." Still smiling, the president of the railroad walked away as the workers closed in around Travis. They wanted to know how he came to be on a first name basis with a railroad president.

Before anyone even asked, Travis said, “We both started working for the railroad on the same day, about 20 years ago.”

“Well, how come he’s president and you still work here in the yard?” three men asked at once.

“Twenty years ago, I came to work for the paycheck; Jim came to work for the railroad.”

Enthusiastic people always look at the broader picture. They see more than people who lack enthusiasm. Who knows what would have happened to Travis if he had come to work for the railroad.

Journal Notes About Enthusiasm: Developing the Qualities of Success

If you learned to be enthusiastic when you were growing up, describe a memory of a family member's enthusiasm that affected you. Also list how different family members' actions showed their enthusiasm.

WAYS I USED THESE ENTHUSIASM LESSONS IN MY OWN LIFE:

If you did not learn how to be enthusiastic while growing up, look within to see how to remedy that situation and list some steps you are going to take. Three weeks later, reflect on how successful you have been and what still needs improvement.

STEP 1: ____

STARTING DATE: ____________________

RESULT THREE WEEKS LATER: ________________________________

STEP 2: ____

STARTING DATE: ____________________

RESULT THREE WEEKS LATER: ________________________________

STEP 3: ______________________________

____

____

____

____

____

____

STARTING DATE: ______________

RESULT THREE WEEKS LATER: ______________

____

____

____

____

____

____

STEP 4: ______________________________

____

____

____

____

____

____

STARTING DATE: ______________

RESULT THREE WEEKS LATER: ______________

____

____

____

____

____

____

Chapter 11

Purpose

His doctors called him very brash, opinionated, willful—they were honest about his chances: "We're going to do the best we can, but you're going to have to win this fight." Before winning the world's premier cycling race in 1999, Lance Armstrong raced neck and neck with death.

Armstrong began 1996 as a cyclist determined to improve; he ended the year with a 40 to 45 percent chance of living. That fall he visited a urologist about a sore testicle and learned he had testicular cancer that already had spread to his lungs. Within 24 hours the cancerous testicle was removed. Armstrong started chemotherapy. Later, golfball-size tumors were removed from his lungs. On the advice of a friend, he requested a brain scan, which revealed two lesions.

An oncologist and amateur cyclist e-mailed his recommendation that Armstrong see the doctors at Indiana University (IU), leaders in the treatment of testicular cancer. Armstrong interviewed the IU doctors and three days later they removed two lesions from his brain. Four five-day bouts of chemotherapy followed. During his 16-day breaks between chemo sessions, Armstrong went home to Austin, where he rode his bike 30 to 50 miles a day.

Since his recovery, Lance Armstrong's sense of purpose has widened, and he has set up the Lance Armstrong Foundation to benefit cancer patients. His Web site provides information about himself and cancer recovery. Armstrong personally answers e-mail from cancer patients and forwards information about them to his doctors. He invites cancer patients to his home for holiday celebrations.

After sitting out 1997 as a year of recovery and renewal, Armstrong re-entered cycling in 1998 and won the Tour de France in 1999.

Doctors chalked up Armstrong's recovery to his "courage and spirit and indomitable will." His doctors also say, "He's a much more sensitive man now, much more concerned with giving back. He's really grown." Armstrong's sense of purpose now includes not only winning but also sharing his good fortune by supporting cancer patients and survivors.

In this chapter, we take a closer look at the importance of having a sense of purpose and how it relates to families, communities, and the business world. You will also meet people like Lance Armstrong who improve our world through their sense of purpose.

Living With a Sense of Purpose

A sense of purpose is what keeps the soul alive; it is our reason to be. It is what teenagers are searching for when they ask themselves, What would be worth doing? What would be valuable? After we look within, the answer comes to us and for the rest of our lives it keeps unfolding as our resolve gets stronger and as we dig deeper.

A sense of purpose is an all-encompassing term that focuses our lives. For example, some people may decide to be peacemakers. This choice is evident as they move from home, where their children are learning to resolve problems without violence, to work, where they are labor mediators or educators. On a community level they help people stop arguing and start cooperating; at little league they help parents relax and enjoy the game; in the voting booth, they vote for people who agree with their peacemaking philosophy.

Remember that your sense of purpose is not a specific purpose for one segment of your life, such as, "I'm going to make a million bucks." My sense of purpose, for instance, directs that my books and my talks and my entire life are in lockstep with my beliefs about my purpose in life. Like you, my sense of purpose comes from deep within; it comes from the value system imprinted on my soul by my parents.

As we go through life, we meet or hear about many people with a sense of purpose, an overriding reason to be. For instance:

- Mark McGwire feels a responsibility as a hero. After he set a home run record in 1998, during spring training 1999 McGwire appeared along the foul lines after almost every game to sign autographs. He says, "I'm trying to live my life karmically right, and I'm going to try to live up to my responsibility as a hero."

- Mother Teresa has died but is hard to forget. Stories keep popping up, like this one: When Pope John Paul II sent her his slightly used limousine, Mother Teresa thanked him graciously. Although she appreciated his generosity—everyone knows how crowded the streets are in Calcutta—she sold the limo and used the proceeds to help the sick and dying.
- Archbishop Desmond Tutu chaired South Africa's Truth and Reconciliation Commission, which promised amnesty to those who confessed the crimes they committed under the apartheid system. These crimes were heartbreaking and often hideous, caused by intolerance and hate. Even though sometimes brought to tears, Tutu remained calm and nonjudgmental as he encouraged each person to confess fully.
- Nancy Reagan has been taking care her husband throughout their long married life. Today she is going through the most difficult time—much worse than when the media taunted her for consulting an astrologer. She tenaciously guards the former president's privacy as he battles Alzheimer's disease.
- Martin Luther King, Jr. dreamed he would die shortly before he was shot; in fact, he preached about his dream the night before his death, urging the congregation to continue working for equality. Despite this premonition, King continued doing what he was called to do.

People with a sense of purpose are self-directed, a characteristic that people with one specific purpose lack. Self-directed kids were the ones you hated in school—they always got right down to work. When the teacher stepped out of the room, they kept working because they wanted to learn. Self-directed people have these things in common:

1. As dreamers, they use their dreams to help themselves stay on track for their purpose. Gerry Sexton, M.D., points out that many people fail to set and achieve goals because they've lost the ability to inspire themselves.
2. As achievers, they focus on what they do best, rather than trying to do lots of things minimally well. Oliver Wendell Holmes observed that "Most people go to their graves with

their music still inside them." I personally respect those who play every note of their music everyday.

3. As responsible people, they own up to their choices and are not controlled by others. While waiting in snarled traffic, they don't strike out at everyone in front of them; they remember they chose this route hoping it would be a shortcut.
4. As people of action, they are undeterred by fear, uncertainty, and change. Do they sometimes puzzle over the consequences if something goes wrong? Sure, but they also realize that because their actions set things into motion, they must take action.
5. As people who recognize that they need other people, they thrive on interdependence. They trust and rely upon others because success demands interdependence.

Purposeful Families

The Hollister Family

The Hollister family found a sense of purpose through Annick Hollister, a fine student, a fast sprinter on the track team, and a stubbornly willful child. To her parents, this 15-year-old seemed pretty normal, until a call from the police awakened them early one morning. Annick was outside of a party howling at the moon and saying she saw God. When they brought her home, she slit her wrists. Although her parents didn't recognize it, this was her first acute episode of schizophrenia.

It took a year before Annick was diagnosed in 1978 as having chronic schizophrenia, an incurable, and at the time untreatable, disease. This disease affects more than one million Americans, who hallucinate and hear tormenting voices that they cannot escape. After a while, Annick refused to attend school. She preferred hitchhiking to the beach, hanging out with older boys, and smoking marijuana. Gradually her condition became worse and her rantings became so violent her parents called the police. Periodically Annick left home with strangers, only to return beaten and half-starved weeks later.

As Annick has struggled with her disease, her family has been there for her. In fact, they have been transformed by it. Her younger sister Meggin has devoted herself to finding the cause of her sister's disease. She received a $60,000 award for her study that could lead to a better understanding of how schizophrenia develops in the brain of a fetus. Meggin explained her motivation this way: "It's too late to rewire Annick's brain. It's too late to erase the 15 years of hell Annick had to go through, but it's not too late to prevent it from happening to someone 20 years from now." Her brother John is a Philadelphia pharmaceutical executive who became interested in medicine because of Annick's illness.

Annick's parents, Hal and Patsy Hollister, have become prominent mental-health advocates. Constance Lieber called them "an extraordinary family that has turned adversity into something positive." Lieber is president of the National Alliance for Research on Schizophrenia and Depression (NARSAD).

Annick now lives in an assisted care complex, is a clerical volunteer, and enjoys creating artwork. Seeing the pleasure Annick derived from her artwork, her parents founded NARSAD Artworks to reproduce and sell artwork by the mentally ill. "You always see your kids growing up and finding a path...that would give something back to the world," explained Patsy. "Annick has done that. She gave us the inspiration for Artworks and she certainly inspired Meggin's profession. And, most important, she's beginning to have pleasure in life."

The Sears Family

William and Martha Sears have a child-centered sense of purpose. It became official when Dr. Sears was only 32 and he was offered the job of chief resident of the largest children's hospital in the world. "It was everything a pediatrician could dream of," Sears admitted when he turned down the position at the Toronto Hospital for Sick Children to spend more time with his own children. "Twenty years from now," he said, "my employer won't remember anything I did. But my kids will." The only thing that bothered him was a nagging suspicion that he had just written himself a sure ticket to obscurity. As it turns out, that hasn't been a problem.

Today Dr. William Sears is one of the nation's leading child-care experts. His *Baby Book* has sold more than 330,000 copies, and he writes a monthly column in *Parenting* magazine. Sears and his wife advocate "attachment parenting," in which parents form "a bond between parent and child as early as the womb and build on that bond for matters of discipline."

Sears is in practice with his two oldest sons in San Clemente and Mission Viejo, Calif. He has no problem admitting that some of his best book material comes from parents. "The secret is to surround yourself with wise parents and to have the humility to learn from them." His wife Martha trained as a nurse and works part time on their books as well as giving childbirth education lessons. Mostly she has stayed home raising their eight children, ages seven to 32, because they agree that parents should spend time with their children in the early years to form attachments.

Purposeful Songs

The Searses' belief in forming strong attachments and the importance of raising children reminds me of "Cat's in the Cradle" by Harry Chapin. As I noted in Chapter 6, I use this song in almost all of my talks, keynote addresses, or seminars because it has such a strong impact. Apparently, a lot of people agree with me that children should come first. In 1974, "Cat's in the Cradle" went to number one and stayed at the top of the charts for approximately 28 weeks. In 1994, a group called Ugly Kid Joe put out a debut album called "In Ugly We Trust." The number one song on that heavy metal album was "Cat's in the Cradle"—that's the version I use when I talk to groups of young people. I have lost count of the teens who have come up to comment that they wish their parents would listen to that song and really get it.

Purposeful Community Life

When a community has a sense of purpose, amazing things can and do happen. Sometimes it just takes one person to spread a good idea around. This is what Carolyn McKenzie has done with her nonprofit program, Soccer in the Streets (SITS). She explains her program like this: "Why soccer? Because it's the fastest growing sport in the world, and African-Americans, Hispanics, and Asians are being left out. In other countries, people of color represent the largest number of people participating. Only in the U.S. is it dominated by suburban Caucasians. My goal is to increase the participation of minorities in a game that has become the athletic argot of middle-class America."

McKenzie has raised $350,000 to give kids something to do and raise their self-esteem through soccer. SITS provides coaching and equipment and pays entry fees into established leagues for urban children. Since 1989, SITS has taught 100,000 urban kids (mostly boys) the basics in a seven-week Soccer 101 program. A new SITS program, Adidas/Coca-Cola Urban Soccer Girl, is getting more minority girls onto playing fields.

Purposeful Work

Balancing Life and Work

A February 1999 survey of 1,000 workers revealed that they believe the most important aspect of a job is the ability to balance work and family life. Aspects that these workers found not as important were job security, quality of the working environment, and relationships with co-workers and supervisors. Other survey tidbits include:

- 95 percent are concerned about spending more time with their families.
- 92 percent want flexibility in work schedules to take care of family needs.
- 88 percent said the amount of stress at work is an important job factor.
- 87 percent were worried about getting enough sleep.

The preceding four concerns indicate that many Americans want to balance their lives so that they can live purposeful lives. The John J. Heldrich Center for Workforce Development at Rutgers University and the Center for Survey Research and Analysis at the University of Connecticut conducted this survey. (For more about balancing your life, see Chapter 7 of *Change Your Attitude*, my first book.)

Now that we have identified the major problem of balancing work and family and life (which by the way is what I am hearing as I travel around the country), let's look at three actions companies can take to help their employees develop a sense of purpose:

1. Companies must replace mission statements that define their purpose as "to increase shareholder wealth" with something closer to "produce a quality service or product that promotes the well-being of the community and provides a working environment conducive to personal growth and creative productivity while increasing shareholder wealth."

2. Companies must rebuild trust with employees who were dispirited by corporate downsizing in the 1980s. Rightsizing taught the workers who survived to be mistrusting and cynical; somehow, they must be turned into workers who have commitment, drive, and energy.

This situation reminds me of 1974, when Curt Flood was playing for the St. Louis Cardinals. Flood went to court to protest that his contract made him a slave to the Cardinals. After he won the case, free agency started in baseball. Today, free agency has spread from sports to the business world, where a tight job market causes many people to act like free agents who go where they can make the most money. They have absolutely no loyalty to their employers. Until companies rebuild trust, there will continue to be a lot of free agents. One company that does not have this problem is Pacific Life Insurance Company, which remain loyal to its employees. They in turn are very loyal to their company.

3. Companies must satisfy the craving for meaning that employees of all ages feel. Many employees want to be of service to something larger than themselves; employees are looking for a sense of purpose at work and in their lives. As mentioned in the last two chapters, this is a desire for unity.

Some companies actually are creating workplaces that not only make a profit but also have a unified vision and a sense of purpose. As you might imagine, this type of change reinvents the whole business paradigm.

Exxon

Exxon began discussing balancing work and home life in 1982, when it introduced a "whole person" model along with a process to help employees explore consciously working at higher levels of the physical, mental, emotional, and spiritual dimensions of their lives. A decade ago, Exxon started offering an "investment excellence" course to help employees link their purpose, principles, and values to job and personal goal setting. Other programs include managing stress, managing personal change, connecting personal purpose to a career path, and using value-centered time management.

Ceridian

After Control Data Corporation was reshaped into Ceridian, it had many fences to mend—not only with investors unhappy about the company's decline, but also with employees who had no reason to feel confident about Ceridian. CEO Lawrence Perlman advocated a new work environment based on helping employees achieve a work-life balance and on recognizing the company's social and community responsibility. This policy allowed flexible hours, compressed workweeks, and telecommuting. Benefits programs also included adoption assistance and child and elder care resources and referral. The company's flexibility allowed many employees to volunteer at local churches and hospitals and at youth, educational, and social organizations. Improving the quality of the workplace has affected Ceridian's bottom line. Between year-end 1991 and 1995, the company's common stock appreciated at an average annual rate of 40 percent. Ceridian is a good client of mine, and they do walk their talk.

Adams and Adams Building Services

John Adams had a difficult time convincing his company that building trust, respect, and caring relationships was important. Adams remembered, "When I started to talk of corporate hugs and corporate love, my staff looked at me as if I were joking. Today these concepts have been embraced by the company to the point that they are a part of our everyday vocabulary and culture. Sure, there are some that may think I'm a bit eccentric, but leadership involves being ahead of the pack. It takes courage to be on the leading edge of change, and good leadership starts with courage and a deep commanding faith in yourself and your higher values."

Medtronic

Medtronic is a medical products company in Minneapolis that knows how to put faces on its employees' sense of purpose. Each year the company has a holiday party for its employees for which it flies in patients, their families, and doctors to share their survival stories. Employees can see exactly how what they do on the job improves people's lives.

While interviewing prospective employees, Medtronic's human resources staff strives to be sure that interviewees have a sense of purpose that matches the company's mission of helping people to live a full life in good health. Employee orientations and leadership courses reinforce the company's mission.

Fel-Pro

Fel-Pro, an automotive product manufacturer in Skokie, Ill., has a simple managerial philosophy: "We treat people the way they should be treated—like people, not numbers." Fel-Pro has been addressing work-family-life issues for more than 25 years. Three of their most outstanding benefits include:

- A free, in-house career counseling program for the purpose of keeping employees and empowering them. Fel-Pro wants to forge a partnership with employees rather than create a paternalistic relationship. Outside consultants are brought in for employees who decide to build their careers elsewhere.
- A year-round day care center for preschool and kindergarten children.
- Tuition reimbursement for outside education that advances an employee's professional development; a $1,000 bonus for employees who complete advanced degrees; scholarships of up to $3,300 per year for four years to any employee's child accepted at an accredited college or trade school; and extensive internal training and improvement programs.

In 1990 researchers from the University of Chicago asked Fel-Pro for permission to do an in-depth study of the bottom line impact of its work-family-life agenda. Researchers began by assessing worker engagement. They measured willingness to participate and cooperate, levels of effort and attention to work, the encouragement of improvement suggestions, and adaptability and willingness to change.

The University of Chicago study revealed that Fel-Pro's work-family-life benefits created a workforce that thrives in a demanding manufacturing environment. In commenting on the study's conclusions, co-president Paul Lehman said:

> They show that employees that participate most in our benefits also have the best work records. They have the fewest disciplinary notices. They have the best quality records.

They participate the most in voluntary teams. They give us the most suggestions for productivity and quality improvement. But, most importantly, they also say that they understand why Fel-Pro has to continue to change. They trust us, and they want to change along with the company. And, in many cases, they provide the leadership for change.

Fel-Pro has been profitable since startup and has a market share that continues to grow. The firm has never had a layoff and has a turnover rate of 1.6 percent, compared to the national average of 9 percent.

Maintaining Your Sense of Purpose

Just as your sense of purpose is honed by the process of living and learning, changes in a major segment of your life may upend your ability to even remember you had a sense of purpose. For example: After a divorce, you wonder if anyone will ever love you and if your children will ever stop blaming you. After moving to a new community, you must not only find your way around but also locate a whole laundry list of new service suppliers. After losing a job, you combine your efforts to find a new position with imagining worst-case scenarios based on a misguided belief that no one will hire you.

Although each of these parts of life is important, work life takes up the majority of our time, so we'll look at two cases in which people faced job loss for different reasons. Their experiences can help you make some serious choices. If you are thinking about making a job change, take time to analyze your current job. Figure out why you are not happy and what it would take to change the situation so you could fulfill your purpose. Also look at related jobs to see how the job fit would be if you transferred. In the following cases, the situations are different, but the message is the same: You can maintain your sense of purpose and express it in your work.

Dawn Coe-Jones

Dawn Coe-Jones was one of Canada's top pro golfers. After joining the Ladies Professional Golf Association in 1984, she rose to 11th in the world during her best year, 1990. Then she had an eight-year slump that she attributes to grief caused by the death of her parents within two years of each other. "My parents were my rock. If things were bad for me on the tour, I could always turn to them."

Realizing that she had to be happier before her golf game would improve, Coe-Jones looked for ways to increase her happiness while on tour. When she married in 1992, she gained a very positive husband, Jimmy Jones. She believes, "There is something to be said for surrounding yourself with as many positive people in your life as possible. In any field, with any successful people, supporters are in the background, helping to foster success." She also hired a new caddie.

Coe-Jones continued rediscovering what she enjoyed about the LPGA tour. Now she is more aware of enjoying what she does for a living and believes everyone should do the same. She has found that simply being around people who enjoy what they are doing is catching.

Coe-Jones mentions having positive support people, relearning to enjoy her job, and rediscovering happiness—all good points to remember when considering whether to make a job change or to improve your job fit.

Lee Grant

Actor Lee Grant earned Academy Award nominations, an Emmy for *Peyton Place*, and an Academy Award for *Shampoo*, but while she was busy on stage and screen, Hollywood decided that young audiences wanted to see young actors. The same held true for television advertisers, who forgot that people over 40 watch television and have money to spend.

Grant admits that it was not easy to go from being a well-known actress to an unemployable one because of her age; being part of a glamorous group of talented but unemployed people was small comfort. She began searching for a new career and offers this advice for people whose careers have temporarily stalled: "Don't let other people stop you from doing something you believe you can and want to do. Being told I can't do something is not something I react to by crawling away."

Grant found a new way to express her creativity: moving behind the camera as a student-director in the first Women's Project at the American Film Institute in 1974. She began producing film features and documentaries. In 1982, she and her husband, Joseph

Fuery, formed a production company that has produced documentaries, a feature film, television movies, and biographies. They won an Academy Award for their study of homelessness, *Down and Out in America*.

Grant has found that the same survival rules apply to all professions: "In jumping from one stone to another, it is vital to seek out a new obsession." She advises re-energizing your career by "staying in there, seeing what turns up next," and believing that you are a survivor. Grant also advises staying busy, even if you have to start slightly lower than you want. Commenting on her own experience, she said: "I think Hollywood was so shocked when I decided to direct that they didn't really open their arms to me as much as they did when I was an actor. So I had to go to New York and start work where I could, usually on documentaries."

Grant reminds people transitioning in the job market to have strong emotional support from close friends and family. She greatly appreciated her husband and longtime colleagues, who reminded her that she could do anything.

Journal Notes About Being Purposeful: Developing the Qualities of Success

Take some time, find some solitude, and contemplate about your individual sense of purpose. After you look within, describe your individual sense of purpose and how it has changed, if it has:

Take an inventory now to see how you're doing. Begin by answering yes or no to these questions, developed by Richard Leider:

Yes	No	
___	___	Do I wake up most Mondays feeling energized to go to work?
___	___	Do I have deep energy—feel a personal calling—for my work?
___	___	Am I clear about how I measure my success as a person?
___	___	Do I use my gifts to add real value to people's lives?
___	___	Do I work with people who honor the values I value?
___	___	Can I speak my truth in my work?
___	___	Am I experiencing true joy in my work?
___	___	Am I making a living doing what I most love to do?
___	___	Can I speak my purpose in one clear sentence?
___	___	Do I go to sleep most nights feeling this was a well-lived day?

Total yes responses _________

If you answered yes all 10 times, go to the next paragraph. If you answered yes fewer than 10 times, how could you change your work so that it does not conflict with your sense of purpose? Write your thoughts below:

Take a look at how you are doing in the rest of your life and write about how each part reflects your sense of purpose:

FAMILY LIFE:

Community Life:

Social Life:

Spiritual Life:

Chapter 12

Improver

Sometimes you hear about something so sad that you just have to do something. That's the way Makenzie Snyder felt when she heard that many foster children had to transport all their possessions in trash bags each time they moved into new homes. Realizing how embarrassing it must be to meet a new family while hauling trash bags, she started collecting used suitcases and duffel bags in her hometown of Bowie, Md.

Through her efforts, a Children-to-Children program in Washington, D.C. distributed suitcases, complete with friendly notes and stuffed animals, to more than 1,000 foster children.

In September of 1999, the Freddie Mac Foundation for Children gave Makenzie Snyder a grant of $15,000 for 1,000 more duffel bags. The following month she was honored at the White House.

And world improver Makenzie Snyder was only 9 years old.

Like young Makenzie Snyder, my father and mother were improvers: They believed they were improving the world by adopting my brother and myself. My folks felt blessed that they could choose two boys—maybe little guys someone else didn't want—and give them a home, guidance, food, clothing, and education. My parents left their legacy by adopting us and giving us lessons in good behavior and leadership along with everything else. Having inherited their desire to improve the world, today I am a Make-A-Wish volunteer, and when my sons played soccer, I coached their teams. My sons are following their grandparents' approach, too, by improving their world.

The previous chapters dealt with looking within to see how to improve yourself. This chapter deals with looking within to improve someone else's world. Looking within and deciding how you can help others is especially important if you are not now making regular contributions of time, talent, or money to charitable organizations.

This chapter also examines a few famous people (as well as some not so famous ones) who are good corporate citizens. They are improving the businesses and the world. This is by no means a listing of all the things people do to improve the world. It is more of a jumping-off point, a thought starter, so that you can appreciate what others have done and follow their extraordinary examples in your own unique way.

Lighting the Way for Others

In his inaugural address on January 20, 1989, George Bush referred to the brightness of a "thousand points of light—of all the community organizations that are spread like stars throughout the nation, doing good." More than a decade later, Americans continue lighting the way for other people and future Americans by donating their time and talents individually or through their employers. Some are helping people who have fallen victim to sudden disasters. Others are helping those who have lost their homes or health. Still others tutor people who lack basic skills. Some are raising money to preserve historical and cultural treasures. Others are helping the disabled. Still others make or deliver meals for the homebound.

In addition to giving their time and talent, Americans are donating money: In 1998, 77 percent of the population and companies contributed more than $174 billion. Before going on, we must answer the question, "Who needs to improve the world anyway?"

Help Yourself

There are more than enough volunteer jobs to go around, so help yourself to one. And that's exactly what you will be doing—helping yourself. The more you give, the more you get back. As essayist Ralph Waldo Emerson wrote, "It is one of the most beautiful compensations of life that no man can seriously help another without helping himself."

A century later, Robert Kennedy wrote, "Few will have the greatness to bend history, but each of us can work to change a small portion of events, and in the total of all those acts will be written the history of this generation....It is from the numberless diverse acts of courage and belief that human history is shaped."

Emerson and Kennedy describe successful people who are world improvers: They are those who help others give themselves reasons to feel proud and they make use of their power to improve our world. Other benefits of volunteering include finding a place to belong, networking, locating people with similar interests, improving career skills, and developing skills unrelated to job skills.

Improving the world is not something for only the over-50 crowd. When people think of all volunteers as gray and retired, they are shortchanging the younger generation. According to public relations consultant David Gergen, Generation X is a generation of volunteers whose numbers are impressive. For example, 10,000 young people applied for 3,500 positions available with the Peace Corps. Teach for America got 3,000 applicants for its 500 positions. And AmeriCorps signed up its 100,000th member at the end of 1998; these young men and women who give at least one year's service to communities.

No matter what your age, consider these suggestions when choosing a volunteer position and/or becoming a regular donor:

➢ Choose something you have a passion for and something you can do.

➢ Investigate your community's needs to see where you can fit in. Some cities have clearinghouses of information about volunteer groups, such as the nonprofit New York Cares. While considering a specific group, check out how much of the organization's budget actually is spent on the participants. United Way and Independent Sector also can provide information.

➢ Arrange to visit the site or agency and talk with a volunteer for a realistic description of what's going on there.

No Guilt Trips

Not everyone has the time, money, mobility, personality, or ability to improve the world. But before you jump to the conclusion that you definitely can't be an improver, finish the chapter and answer the questions in the journaling section. These can generate ideas about what you can do. Then, look within to determine what you should do.

People Who Change the World

Ordinary world improvers come in all shapes, sizes, ages, colors, and religions. Consider the grandparents who shelter and raise their children's children. Improvers also visit the sick, tutor students, chauffeur those who can't drive, pick up litter, paint murals over graffiti, and take a stand against prejudice. As the following stories show, they believe that they can make a difference and that they are empowered to improve the world.

Richie Stochowski

When he was just 11, Richie was scuba diving with his father when he came up with a million-dollar idea: Water Talkies that enable divers to communicate while under water. On the way home from vacation, Richie began drawing sketches of his invention. Back in California, his father helped him develop a model and his mother accompanied him to a meeting with Toys 'R Us. Since then Richie has invented several other water toys and sold his company, Short Stack, for $1 million.

Just before the sale, 13-year-old Richie visited the National Gallery of Young Inventors in Akron and decided to help other young people who were inventors. He issued a challenge to companies to establish a $100,000 fund to be divided among three nonprofit organizations that encourage children to innovate and incorporate. Richie donated $1,000 and challenged 10 other companies to donate $10,000 each.

Bob Thompson

Bob Thompson started an asphalt company 40 years ago in the basement of his Belleville, Mich. home with $3,500. His wife supported them by teaching school. A few years later he enlarged his asphalt company to include road building. In July of 1999, Thompson sold the business for $442 million and gave $128 million to improve the lives of his 550 workers—the salespeople, secretaries, gravel pit guys, and road sign gals.

Thompson said he did this because these "people worked exceedingly hard for us." He pointed out that his company's success was built by these good workers, who sometimes worked 14-hour days and six-day weeks in blisteringly hot weather with 300-degree asphalt. Thompson figured he was just being fair to his employees.

"A lot of people don't get the opportunity [to do what I did], but would if they could," he says. "This didn't change my life a whole lot, when you get right down to it." Salaried workers received checks or annuity certificates ranging from $1 to $2 million to be cashed in at age 55 or 62. Some of the checks hourly workers received—$2,000 for each year of service—were larger than their annual salaries. Thompson included some retirees and widows in his plan and even paid the taxes of $25 million. Thompson, who lives modestly, also plans to give away the rest of his fortune. He began by setting up a trust for the education of inner-city children.

Regina Jennings

Regina Jennings waited tables, mopped floors, and scrubbed bathrooms as a cleaning lady at West Virginia University's College of Law in Morgantown from 1974 to 1982. She earned less than $10,000 a year. Still, Jennings managed to save and invest her wages, as well as the money she collected on rental property.

In April 1999, Jennings returned to Morgantown for the dedication of the $93,000 Regina Jennings Distance Learning and Teleconferencing Room, which allows the college to broadcast courses statewide. Retired for 10 years, Jennings said, "I always wanted [to do] something that would help the students."

Margaret Gallimore

Margaret Gallimore cares and understands. A private duty nurse, she moved her children to Dallas so she could care for an aunt who had cancer. In 1986, she noticed the number of homeless men in the depressed area where her aunt lived, so she rented the house next door as a homeless shelter for men. When the local AIDS clinic closed, she turned her homeless shelter into an AIDS hospice named for her aunt. Mathis Hospice is a labor of love that

Gallimore supports by providing private duty care; a friend helps with a regular monthly donation.

Gallimore says, "We're a family at Mathis Hospice. I do the cooking and clean house. I nurse them and give them baths. I take them for rides in my car so they can have a change of scene and get some fresh air."

Why does she do this? Her answer is that "It's God-given. The good Lord made me this way. I can't stand to see people suffer....As a kid I wanted to be a missionary and take the faith to foreign lands. They tell me I'm doing my missionary work now. I've been their father, their mother, and their brother. I bathe them when they are dying; I feed them."

Philip Vera Cruz

Born in the Philippines, Vera Cruz arrived in Seattle in 1926. "All the stories we heard were only success stories," he says. "So my plan was to finish college in America, get a good job...save my money, and return home and support my family. It was only after I finally got to America that I understood how different reality was for us Filipinos."

For 40 years, Vera Cruz worked in canneries and at seasonal field jobs in the western United States. In 1965 he joined the United Farm Workers (UFW) and later became the union's vice president. For his lifelong service to the Filipino community in America, Vera Cruz received the first Ninoy M. Aquino Award in 1987. Part of this award made possible his first trip back to the Philippines, where he was greeted by the family he worked so hard to support. In describing this trip, he said, "My brother and sister got good educations and they succeeded in providing their children with a good education. That's important to me because I made it possible for them."

Vera Cruz's desire to improve the world served him, his family, and his people well. Through it all, he remained a dreamer: "If I could inspire one or two young people to be successful by hearing my story....If these one or two young people might turn into someone who could help change history....If more young people could just get involved in the important issues of social justice, they would form a golden foundation for the struggle of all people to improve their lives."

Well-Known Improvers

All of the following well-known people have taken advantage of their fame to make a difference in the lives of others.

Colin Powell

These days, former chief of staff General Colin Powell spends more than half of his time improving the lives of children in his program, America's Promise—The Alliance for Youth. The goals of this program are to see that each child at risk has:

1. A healthy start.
2. An ongoing relationship with a caring adult (mentor, tutor, coach).
3. A safe place and structured activities after school (15 million are now alone between 3 and 8 p.m., which is when juvenile crime soars).
4. A marketable skill as a result of efficient education.
5. A chance to help others through community service.

You probably remember the TV coverage of President Bill Clinton's summit on volunteerism in 1997 at Independence Hall in Philadelphia; it was a great media opportunity for mayors, governors, former presidents, politicians, and celebrities, who all exuded good will, as did corporate representatives. If cynical viewers wondered just how long all this cooperation for America's Promise would last, they sold Colin Powell short. That day he seriously asked "every single person who has been successful to give some of their time, talent, and money to help a child in need." Successful people have responded by pledging not only millions of dollars but also millions of hours. In its second year, America's Promise touched 10.3 million children. The value of these commitments is estimated at $295.5 million.

Powell travels around the country holding everyone's feet to the fire. He has no problem reminding groups of their promises as he visits more than 600 promise partners (business and community groups) throughout the country. In addition to cheerleading, fund-raising, and giving speeches to adults, Powell makes time to talk with children wherever he goes. The retired general also has adopted Macfarland Middle School in Washington, D.C., where he drops in for lunch with the kids when he's in town. If you would like to learn about volunteer opportunities with America's Promise in your community, go to *www.americaspromise.org*.

Paul Newman

Actor Paul Newman makes more money with his food than with his films. His company, Newman's Own, donates 100 percent of after-tax profits to charitable and educational causes around the world. Since 1982, this has totaled $100 million.

Doug Flutie

Taking a page out of Newman's playbook, this quarterback with the Buffalo Bills has used his name to sell cereal, candy bars, and submarine sandwiches. All proceeds go to the Doug Flutie Jr. Autism Foundation to improve the lives of his son and other autistic children.

Dolly Parton

Tennessee native, country singer, and actor Dolly Parton hasn't forgotten how it feels to grow up poor, and she puts her money where her heart is. She turned an amusement/entertainment park in her hometown, Pigeon Forge, into Dollywood, one of the state's top attractions. More than 11 million tourists have boosted the area's employment rate by spending $615 million there each year.

Parton also began helping to improve the literacy rate of Sevier County, where two out of five adults lack a high school diploma and one child in five lives in poverty. Through her Dollywood Foundation, Parton is putting books into the hands of children—5,200 children in 1998, at $350 a head. Each child receives one book every month from birth until age 5, and 70 percent of preschoolers in the county are enrolled. Parton plans to spend $1 million over the next five years on her Imagination Library program, which even provides a bookcase for each child's books. Parton notes that the Imagination Library program "is doing what we hoped it would, inspiring children to read more, to learn more, to do more, to be more."

Improvement-Oriented Companies

Corporate charity isn't a new idea. For example, the Ronald McDonald House Charities began in 1974. In the 1980s, however, leveraged buyouts and hostile takeovers caused cuts in corporate charity. But by the booming late 1990s, corporate citizenship had rebounded. According to the Points of Light Foundation, 1,500 companies were members of volunteer councils, compared to 600 in 1985. A 1992 survey of 454 corporations found that nine out of 10 actively encouraged employees to volunteer.

Companies with community service programs have discovered they attract better employees. In fact, a 1996 survey of 2,100 M.B.A. graduates found that when deciding between two equal job offers, 83 percent would choose to work for the more socially responsible company. Some corporate service programs involve an activity for National Volunteer Week, such as cleaning up a few miles of roadside or creating a Web site for a nonprofit organization. Other corporate programs make a longer commitment, such as being a weekly reading tutor or mentoring at-risk youth.

Managers have noticed another advantage of corporate community service programs: Volunteering often improves employees' skills and their spirit of teamwork. Joel Barthelemy, CEO of PAR Technologies, comments, "When we were building walls for Habitat [for Humanity], walls were being broken down between departments. No longer was sales the enemy of accounting, credit, and collection. When everybody is pitching in like that, you build enormous team spirit and respect." Several companies that I have worked with are involved with Habitat; all of them say that building houses has not only increased the teamwork of their staff, but also their self-esteem. The more they give, the more they get back.

Because customers buy products from companies that are good citizens, retailers also are advertising their community involvement. A 1999 Cone/Roper Cause Related Marketing Trends Report found that if the prices and product quality were equal, two-thirds of Americans would buy the product of a company pushing a good cause. And 68 percent of those would even pay more for products linked to good causes. An obvious example is Newman's Own foods.

Target Corporation (formerly known as Dayton Hudson Corporation) found its record of corporate generosity paid off in 1987 when fending off Dart Corporation's attempted unfriendly takeover. The Minnesota legislature passed a state law that eliminated unfriendly takeovers undoubtedly in part because of Dayton Hudson's generosity in its home state. Equally important, the retailer's institutional stockholders fully supported the legislature's efforts. Accordingly, Dayton Hudson has updated its low-key approach. Today ads explain its charitable activities, as do special product stickers at Target discount stores. These remind consumers that 5 percent of pre-tax annual profits go directly back to Target communities.

Wal-Mart

Consumers chose Wal-Mart as the nation's most socially responsible company in 1998, dethroning McDonald's, which had held that top position since 1993. Wal-Mart contributed $127.9 million to local community programs involving education, family issues, and children.

Liz Claiborne

Liz Claiborne has been fighting domestic violence since 1991 by spearheading a national campaign using billboards, TV ads, posters, brochures, workshops, and partnerships with local retailers. The firm's managers believe this initiative fulfills its responsibility to the people who make its stores successful. According to Jan Randel, director of Women's Work: "We don't link [our philanthropic program] to how it affects sales—that's not what it's all about. But we can't have a healthy business without healthy consumers, and to the degree this program propels that thought, it's good for business."

Liz Claiborne also donates profits from special items to the Family Violence Prevention Fund and a percentage of store sales to local agencies during Domestic Violence Awareness Month in October.

Timberland

Jeff Schwartz, Timberland's CEO, believes that "Doing well and doing good are inextricably linked." This apparel and footwear firm supports City Year, a program in 10 cities for young people who devote a year of service to their communities. Timberland has donated $8 million to City Year and, as the official apparel supplier, has outfitted 4,000 members.

Levy Restaurants

The Levy Cares charity efforts of Levy Restaurants in St. Louis have included supporting Our Little Haven, a residential treatment facility for infants and children up to age 5 who have been abused, neglected, or exposed to drugs or HIV. For example, Levy employees brought picnic lunches and catered the dedication of the new Baby Building.

In Washington, D.C., Levy employees do grocery shopping, stock shelves, and deliver 1,500 meals for Open Hand. They also offer computer classes to men of all ages at Pacific Garden Mission. In Kansas City, the staff cooks and serves lunch at the Arrowhead Club for children in the big brothers and big sisters program, as well as partnering with them.

Like Timberland, other companies are funneling their charitable efforts into consumer-related areas. For example,

- Whirlpool's chief customers are women; accordingly, the firm contributes to child care programs and job training for women.
- Avon, the cosmetics company, channels donations to breast cancer researchers.
- Kimberly-Clark makes paper products, including diapers, and has helped fund playgrounds in economically depressed neighborhoods.
- Fuller Plumbing, a five-employee firm in Chula Vista, California, does plumbing repairs for the needy during slow periods, which decreased considerably when local papers published their story.

If you work for a company that has a corporate charity arm, it is a lot easier to donate time and to find the right place to volunteer. If you own a company that does not make donations of time, talent, and money, please consider the benefits of doing so. We really do need to improve our world because we benefit so much from helping others. It's like a boomerang—when we give, we get so much more back. Use the journaling section to get started.

Journal Notes About Being an Improver: Developing the Qualities of Success

Once again, it's time to look within to identify how you can improve the world. Review the values you listed in the journaling section of Chapter 11 and choose several activities (or just one) that would have an impact not only on your world, but also on the world around you. Enter these values and related activities below and describe why you chose them.

FIRST VALUE: ______________________

ACTIVITY: ______________________

____

____

CHOSEN BECAUSE: ______________________

____

____

SECOND VALUE: ______________________

ACTIVITY: ______________________

____

____

CHOSEN BECAUSE: ______________________

____

____

THIRD VALUE: ______________________

ACTIVITY: ______________________

____

____

CHOSEN BECAUSE: ______________________

____

____

To help you decide whether you want to volunteer, donate money, or both, look within as you read the following questions from Jim Brosseau and answer yes or no.

_____ 1. Do you have the time to serve weekly or biweekly without decreasing time now devoted to your family, career, or other commitments?

_____ 2. Could your family volunteer as a family activity?

_____ 3. Would you get too emotional being around seriously ill or disabled children, homeless people, or Alzheimer's patients?

_____ 4. Does this activity reflect your interests, temperament, and politics?

_____ 5. Are you doing this out of guilt because your company encourages volunteerism or because most of your friends or co-workers are volunteers?

_____ 6. Can you accept the fact that volunteering isn't always fun?

_____ 7. Would you feel safe in the neighborhood or facility where you would be volunteering?

_____ 8. Could you observe the activity before making a long-term commitment to it?

_____ 9. Can you accept the way an agency's rules define a volunteer's role?

_____ 10. Can you resist trying to save the world and settle for making a corner of it a better place?

After investigating each activity and looking within, describe your conclusion for each—whether you are still interested in contributing your time, talent, and money and why.

FIRST ACTIVITY: ______________________________

____

____

____

____

____

SECOND ACTIVITY ______________________________

THIRD ACTIVITY: ______________________________

____

____

____

____

____

____

If you want to be an improver, but can't donate time, talent, or money just now, don't give up. Do one good deed each day—just one—and amaze yourself with the feeling of joy you get from improving the world around you. Say hello to people you see often; don't wait for a formal introduction. Smile at people. Call your waiter or sales clerk by name. Put a piece of litter in a trash can to improve your community. It all adds up.

Chapter 13

Spiritual

You've probably seen the classic photo of cars driving through an opening in a sequoia in California's Muir Woods National Monument. How did this group of giant trees escape being turned into 100 subdivision homes and a zillion toothpicks? You can credit John Muir and a nudge from God.

John Muir's family immigrated to Wisconsin from Scotland in 1849, when he was 11. As he was growing up, Muir was not only fascinated by nature but also enjoyed hand-carving clocks and creating barometers, hydrometers, and table saws. Later, working as an inventor of farm implements, Muir was temporarily blinded by a factory accident.

After recuperating, Muir used his recovered sight to become a wilderness explorer, naturalist, and conservationist. "I bade adieu to all my mechanical inventions," he wrote, "determined to devote the rest of my life to study the inventions of God." And so, he became a wanderer and a wonderer, beginning with a 1,000-mile walk to Florida. He then traveled to Cuba and eventually arrived in the Yosemite Valley.

As he explored America's West Coast all the way to Alaska, Muir began writing articles about the beauty of Yosemite and urging government protection of the forests. He also wrote books, lectured about his travels throughout the world, and co-founded the Sierra Club in 1895. Reflecting on his life-changing blindness, Muir wrote: "God has to nearly kill us sometimes to teach us lessons."

Fortunately, many of us escape life-changing experiences like John Muir's. More often, it is a nagging feeling that we should be doing something else that drives us to take action. God meets us where we are—even when we're hiding—so we might as well do what the voice inside tells us to do, because it's not going away. In this chapter, we look at the spiritual side of life, meet some people like Muir whose lives were changed, and discuss the physical and emotional benefits of spirituality.

Although I do not advocate any specific religious beliefs, I feel that you must look within to find your own spirituality and to find a place and time for God in your life. This description from David Elkins pretty well describes my take on the width and breadth of spirituality: "From the rain dances of Native Americans to the celebratory dances of Hasidic Jews, from the whirling dervishes of Islam to the meditating monks of Zen Buddhism, from the ecstatic worship services of charismatic churches to the solemn, silent meetings of the Quakers, spirituality takes on many expressions."

This final chapter complements the previous chapter about improving our world. I was reminded of the importance and intertwined relationship between spirituality and improving the world not long ago, when I spoke to the Young Presidents Organization (YPO). All of the organization's members became company presidents before the age of 40. A recent survey of the membership revealed that the majority believed that spirituality and improving our world were necessary ingredients of success.

Become Spiritual

Spiritual people have a sense of humility; they believe that a Higher Power or God is more important than themselves. Spirituality has as many facets as a well-cut diamond. Spirituality means orienting ourselves to our world so that we are in awe, wonder, and amazement at the splendor of the universe. Some describe their spirituality as stressing the unity of all human beings and the unity of all being. For others, it is networking with God. For still others, it is being aware of our connection to God, the Earth, and others. It is also understanding our place in the universe. For all of us, spirituality nourishes the flame of the spirit within.

In the first chapter, I discussed the Delany sisters' self-discipline, a trait which is necessary to becoming spiritual. Sadie mentioned that she and Bessie set aside some time to talk to the Lord each day. She added:

We got that habit from Mama. She had a full-time job running the school, plus 10 children to raise, but there was never a day in her life that she didn't reserve one full hour to pray. She had a beautiful writing desk where she kept her special things, like her own Bible and prayer book. Above it were two pictures of her heroes—Abraham Lincoln and Frederick Douglass—and when she sat down between them, we knew we had to leave her alone. That was her hour with the Lord.

Today we have Mama's writing desk in our living room and I keep those two pictures over my bed. They remind us that no one is ever too busy or pressured or tired to make a time and place for God in their lives. After all, He has to manage the whole world, and He's never too busy for us.

Sadie Delany makes several good points about developing our spirituality, such as establishing a time and place for listening to God. Although a lot of people can talk on their cell phones while negotiating traffic, don't even consider trying to drive and listen to God at the same time—there's far too much static. Instead, choose prime time to give God all of your attention. You can either choose a time with few distractions or invite your family to join you in making time for God. Like the Delanys did, your children will learn from your actions.

You may want to designate a special place in your home where you can talk to God, or, like Henry David Thoreau, you may prefer the outdoors. While living at Walden Pond, Thoreau found nature to be a temple of God and source of life. If you are an outdoors person, take a walk or run in a quiet park. Take some deep, relaxing breaths and allow yourself to become more and more aware of your body, nature, and God as you move along. If you enjoy the outdoors, choose a spot where you can be alone with your Higher Power. But no matter where you choose, just be sure to make a place and time for God.

Rabbi Harold Kushner, author of *When Bad Things Happen to Good People,* compares our spiritual growth to climbing a ladder. "We climb up slowly, step by step. With each step we take, we solidify our footing, then move on to the next one. Each step nourishes our soul. In time we will feel completely nourished and connected to God. We will have truly met God."

Mixed Messages About Spirituality

We hear about the necessity of people sustaining their spiritual lives just about every week:

- National polls indicate that 90 percent of Americans believe in God or a Higher Power.
- The Gallup Organization released a July 14, 1999, survey about religion based on interviews with more than 40,000 Americans. Researchers asked: How important is religion in your life? Those answering "very important" included:
  - 45 percent of 18- to 29-year-olds.
  - 55 percent of those 30 to 49.
  - 70 percent of 50- to 74-year-olds.
  - 77 percent of those over 75.

  Note that the closer we get to meeting God, the more spiritual we become.
- More than 200 educators from 35 countries met in October of 1999 at the University of Cincinnati to discuss teaching morality and spirituality to decrease the spread of violence. Their comments indicate the need for spirituality. A representative from India said: "Moral and spiritual values must be included in education along with rationality. By that I don't mean a particular religion, but a belief in something beyond one's own self-interests." A representative from Tibet said: "I would attribute [the low incidence of violence in Tibetan schools] to our culture, which is based on the Buddhist principles of compassion, love, and kindness. Our children get cultural and religious instruction from their parents and from the schools."
- Coach Mike Ditka commented that society is going downhill: "If people abided by the first two of the 10 Commandments, we wouldn't have near the problems we have in our society today....We've taken God out of our society, out of government, out of the schools. As a result, we've had a big deterioration....There is a right and there is a wrong, and it's not so much based on the laws of man, it's based on the laws of God."

I agree with Ditka wholeheartedly. Doing a little research, I found there are more than 34 million laws in this country. I believe we could do away with all of them if we paid attention to the 10 original laws. The more we keep spirituality out of our lives, the more laws we are going to need.

The message of God's love for us seems to have gotten lost as we are bombarded by mixed messages about spirituality: Yes, God is important to us and we will attend a prayer breakfast—where we can network to improve business—but God is not important enough to receive daily attention. More important is the message our children get by watching our actions. We may say we believe in God, but if we don't put our belief into action, it's like driving a five-speed car using only first gear. We are not using all of our potential when we don't make a time and place for God in our lives. So many of society's problems today could be solved if we could increase the percentage of people who not only believe in God but also take advantage of God's daily 24-hour open house.

Spirituality can change our lives, our children's lives, and our communities, so let's look at the benefits to becoming spiritual.

Benefits of Spirituality

Spiritual Traits

Motivational speaker and author Donna Rae Smith has found that many successful, spiritually centered businesspeople have specific characteristics. I've paraphrased her list to show that these traits also can benefit families, neighborhoods, schools, and communities. While becoming a spiritual person is not a quick fix, this life-affirming change is worth the wait because it affects everyone we meet or talk with in so many ways. Developing our spiritual natures causes us to:

- Serve others by improving their lives and finding better ways to communicate with them.
- Listen with our hearts because we learn by listening.
- Cheerlead to help others experience life's delight, joy, and surprise.
- Find the good in others' actions.

- ➢ Offer forgiveness by understanding rather than judging.
- ➢ Build others' self-esteem.
- ➢ Walk our talk to align our actions with our stated beliefs.
- ➢ Encourage and praise excellence in others.

Health

God has given our bodies a natural inclination to survive, a healing power that is our life force. Sometimes, our beliefs, emotions, and behavior can decimate that life force rather than enhancing it. When that happens, we need to straighten out our life force, just like we must straighten out a twisted hose before watering the garden. The spiritual interventions of others and the development of our own spiritual lives straighten out our life force, enabling it to heal us.

Psychotherapist David N. Elkins believes that spirituality is essential to human happiness and mental health. Elkins writes that when passion and depth are missing in our lives, spirituality can help us find them. He reminds us that psychologists such as William James, Gordon Allport, Erich Fromm, Viktor Frankl, Abraham Maslow, and Rollo May have focused on spirituality in their work. Carl Jung also found that spirituality was essential to psychological health. Currently many psychologists agree that spirituality plays a role in their patients' mental health.

Through research over many years, Dr. Herbert Benson has documented that daily meditation—which is a part of spirituality—can reduce stress and promote relaxation and overall well-being. Today 60 medical schools offer spirituality and healing classes for medical personnel; this is quite an increase from five years ago, when only three schools offered such courses.

In 1995, *Good Morning America* had a five-part segment about the connection between medicine and spirituality. They offered substantial proof from hospitals and doctors throughout the nation who had studied this relationship and concluded that when patients' families had a belief in God and prayed, the recovery rate was higher, mortality rate was lower, and attitudes were better. Doctors noted that patients who believed in a Higher Power recovered more quickly, got over their illnesses, bounced back more readily, and were more open to fighting the illness.

I found this to be very powerful material because I've seen a lot of spirituality in families that I meet through Make-A-Wish. They don't always say formal prayers aloud, but I see them bowing their heads, holding a sleeping child's hand, and know they are praying.

Deepak Chopra and Wayne Dyer put together a set of tapes titled *Living Beyond Miracles*. On those tapes, Dyer points out that years ago if you asked whether a scientist believed in God, the scientist would respond, "Of course not, I am a scientist." Today, however, the answer is, "Sure I do, I'm a scientist." How wonderful to see such a change in society.

Although researchers have conducted relatively few studies about the advantages of spirituality, the Alameda County Study, which monitors 7,000 Californians, indicated spiritual people had "markedly less stress over finances, health, and other daily concerns than non-spiritual types." Other studies have found that spiritual people have lower blood pressure, faster recovery from illness, a lower mortality rate, better immunity, and less depression than non-spiritual people. A review of additional studies linked spirituality with low suicide rates, less alcohol and drug abuse, less criminal behavior, fewer divorces, and greater marital satisfaction. I haven't conducted any scientific studies similar to the preceding ones, but I've found that spiritual people can roll with the punches better than those who haven't looked within to find a time and place to meet daily with their Higher Power.

Rolling with the Punches

When we talk to our Higher Power, there are times we are tempted to say, "Okay, that's enough, this all I can take, get me out of this situation." But God doesn't do that; God gives us the strength to deal with the problem. As an example, Harold Kushner describes meeting a woman whose daughter's body had rejected three transplanted kidneys. Despite being in kidney failure, the daughter was coping beautifully, remained cheerful, and seemed full of life. Her connection with God helped her meet the challenge of her illness. The mother's spirituality allowed her to appreciate the holiness in her daughter's situation.

It takes more work to keep God out of your life than it does to open up your life and let the goodness of God in. I am noticing many people who are facing trials and have turned over their problems, frustrations, and pain to God. I see them center themselves and look within to meet with God. They get a grip on the reality of their lives and focus on what is really important to them. Too many times we wait until a crisis to turn to God. But don't wait for a crisis—all of the answers are inside if we open our hearts and minds.

Bernie Siegel points out that when we place an order with God, unlike an order at the local pizza parlor, it may not be filled because prayer is not "a test of God, but a call for help to find your inner strength and talent." Siegel reminds us that "we all have the capability to endure whatever comes our way because we are all made of divine stuff." Of course, even though we are made of divine stuff, life can be tough, as the following stories show.

Pete Swet

In 1992 Pete Swet wrote TV plays, soap operas, and comedy; he also wrote for *Sesame Street* and magazines. Life was good until a brain hemorrhage garbled his speech and stiffened his left side. After emergency surgery, a 15-day coma, and two months in the hospital, Swet spent more time in a rehabilitation facility. Today he walks with a limp, his left hand is paralyzed, and his concentration is sometimes bad. "It's like my mind is playing two movie screens at one time and I can't figure out which one to watch," he says. During recovery, Swet's major worry was whether he would be able to write. While overcoming his physical and mental problems, Swet had a book published about his recovery experiences; he also has written a novel and is working on a book about spirituality.

When he was 19, Swet decided there was no God. "That stayed with me almost my whole life," he says, "until I was, like St. Paul, knocked off my high horse and battered around a little bit." During surgery to repair his brain hemorrhage, Swet found himself in a waiting room with other "shades" or souls; at a distance he could see a beautiful, yellow-lit garden. Then he was drawn into a dark alcove for a judgment meeting. That experience, he writes, "was a transcendent moment of mystery and glory, hope and promise, and love—a love I had never known, a love so powerful that it would stay with me when [I was] brought back into the conscious world."

Robert Edwards

As a New England Patriots running back who had a sensational NFL rookie season, including nine touchdowns and 1,115 yards rushing, Robert Edwards was living the good life. But everything changed in February of 1999 on a Hawaiian beach before the Pro Bowl, when he badly dislocated his left knee while playing touch football.

This was another in a string of challenges for Edwards—as a child he was so knock-kneed that doctors were certain he could never play sports. While being touted as a Heisman Trophy candidate during his junior year at Georgia State, Edwards fractured his left foot, though he was fortunate enough to recover and play his senior year. "All my life, I've thrived on people saying, 'He can't do it,'" Edwards says. "If you give up believing you'll get better, it's a lost cause. Accept the fact that you got hurt. Have faith that you'll be completely healthy one day. Tell yourself that miracles happen all the time." By fall of 1999, it seemed as though Edwards would need a miracle to return to football; he walked with a limp and was still undergoing physical therapy.

Edwards's attitude reflects his spirituality: "I'd like to build off my rookie year, but if I'm to be a messenger in another arena, so be it. I'll fight until the end. And I won't stop until I take my last breath. Whatever the plan is for me, I know it'll be something better."

Journal Notes About Being Spiritual: Developing the Quality of Success

Once again it's time to bite the bullet, to make some decisions that can turn your dreams into reality. Begin by describing why your goal for developing spirituality; plan to review this goal periodically to see if your goal and God's plan for you are in sync. For instance, you may ask to be kinder and less cynical about other people but upon reflection you may find that you are listening more. At this point you can either push your agenda, or accept God's gentle shove toward listening more and talking less.

Once you know why, work on when and where you can listen to God. Also be sure to look at the how. If you are going at life full tilt and suddenly skid to a stop for some time with God, you need to plan transitions before and after your God time. Some people use relaxation techniques or breathing exercises to quiet themselves. Christians may say the "Our Father" or another formal prayer. Or, you may choose to repeat a single word or phrase, such as "love" or "peace" or "thanks God."

You also need a plan to stifle disruptions—such as blood-curdling screams from your children, the doorbell, the phone, and your pager.

WHY: ____

When: ______

Where: ______

How: ______

Disruption Avoidance: ______

Epilogue

As a youngster growing up, I remember watching a TV program that featured an epilogue each week. Ever since then, an epilogue has been something special for me, a time to review, to sum up, to create one of those "aha" moments of delight and enlightenment.

To begin, let's review the most important ideas we have discussed:

1. Most successful people are disciplined and self-confident. So if you don't know exactly which traits to begin with, these could be your starting place—but only after looking within, because your life could require entirely different traits.
2. Additional traits of success include being persistent, progressive, decisive, focused, and visionary.
3. Many successful people are lucky, enthusiastic, purposeful, and spiritual; they are also improvers who excel.
4. Most successful people were not born with the 13 traits of success, so they intuitively developed those traits they needed. In other words, they looked within, identified a trait they needed, achieved it, and looked within again.
5. Each person must look within to learn which traits to develop because personal success comes from within. I can give you the recipe, but you have to cook up the stew yourself.
6. The choice is yours—you can look within or do without.

If you have read this far, obviously you are interested in self-improvement and achieving personal success. You most likely have thought about successful people you know and figured out which of the 13 traits they possess.

Perhaps as you were reading you even felt drawn to some traits more than others:

➢ When you read about enthusiasm you may have thought, "I can do that, I could be more enthusiastic."

➢ When you read about being focused, you may have thought, "I should do that, my life is just drifting along with nobody in charge. I've never done anything like this before, but now it just seems right."

➢ When you read about being an improver, perhaps you decided, "I want to do that. I really want to improve my world. Yes, I can do this one. I'm not a rocket scientist, but I don't have to be. I can do it."

If you read through the book without journaling or looking within because you wanted to get the whole picture, now is the time to go back and choose action rather than ignorance. It's time to look within and act upon your insights. What you make of your life is up to you. Just remember that your answers to life's questions lie inside of you. Begin by journaling and looking within to discover which traits you should work on.

If you began looking within and journaling as you read, congratulations. You have chosen personal success. You began looking within and doing something to change your life. You took responsibility for your choices and became accountable for the results. By looking within, you began a wonderful, continuous journey during which you will learn your personal lessons of life.

The benefits of looking within, of learning and growing, are unlimited. It takes courage to look within; it takes honesty to choose to look within. Your life is too valuable not to look within.

Why would you choose to do without?

Suggested Reading

Chopra, Deepak. *Creating Affluence: The A to Z Steps for a Richer Life.* San Rafael, Calif.: Amber-Allen, 1993.

———. *The Seven Spiritual Laws of Success: A Practical Guide to the Fulfillment of Your Dreams.* San Rafael, Calif.: Amber-Allen, 1994.

Collins, James C., and Jerry I. Porras. *Built to Last: Successful Habits of Visionary Companies.* New York: Harper Business, 1994.

Dyer, Wayne, and Deepak Chopra. *How to Get What You Really Really Really Really Want.* Carlsbad, Calif.: Hay House, 1998.

Johnson, Spencer. *The Precious Present.* Garden City, N.Y.: Doubleday, 1984.

Lindberg, Ann Morrow. *A Gift from the Sea.* New York: Pantheon, 1955.

McGraw, Phillip. *Life Strategies.* New York: Simon and Schuster, 1998.

Millman, Dan. *Way of the Peaceful Warrior: A Book That Changes Lives.* Tiburon, Calif.: H. J. Kramer Audio, 1988.

Vanzant, Iyanla. *In the Meantime.* New York: Simon and Schuster, 1998.

Walsch, Neale Donald. *Conversations with God.* Vol. 1. New York: G. P. Putnam's Sons, 1996.

———. *Conversations with God.* Vol. 2. San Bruno, Calif.: Audio Literature, 1997.

———. *Conversations with God.* Vol. 3. San Bruno, Calif.: Audio Literature, 1998.

Williamson, Marrianne. *Return to Love.* New York: Harper Perennial, 1996.

Bibliography

Chapter 1

Bay, Tom, and David Macpherson. *Change Your Attitude.* Franklin Lakes, N.J.: Career Press, 1998.

Delany, Sarah, and A. Elizabeth Delany, with Amy Hill Hearth. *The Delany Sisters' Book of Everyday Wisdom.* New York: Kodansha America, 1994.

"Hall of Fame," *Hawaii Business,* January 1995.

"Harvard Business School Survey of Successful People," *U.S. News and World Report*, June 12, 1988.

Pitino, Rick. *Success Is a Choice.* New York: Broadway Books, 1998.

Siegel, Bernie. *Prescriptions for Living.* New York: HarperCollins, 1998.

Waggoner, Martha. "Delany Sisters an Inspiration to Actresses," *The Columbus Dispatch*, April 6, 1999.

Who's Who in America. Chicago: A. N. Marquis, 1999.

Chapter 2

Bay, Tom, and David Macpherson. *Change Your Attitude.* Franklin Lakes, N.J.: Career Press, 1998.

Branden, Nathaniel. *The Power of Self-Confidence.* Deerfield Beach, Fla.: Health Communications, 1992.

Gloekler, Jacob. "Teaching Kids to Aim High," *University of Dayton Quarterly,* Spring 1999.

Neergaard, Lauran. "Incidence of Breast Cancer Among Men Is on the Rise," *The Columbus Dispatch*, May 9, 1999.

Pitino, Rick. *Success Is a Choice.* New York: Broadway Books, 1998.

Smith, Donna Rae. *The Power of Building Your Bright Side.* Grand Rapids, Mich.: Wynwood, 1995.

Chapter 3

Ashabranner, Brent. *People Who Make a Difference.* New York: E. P. Dutton, 1989.

Bannist, Nicholas. "Unofficially, Its Uses Are Endless," *The Guardian,* May 16, 1999.

Figel, Marge. "Are You Persistent or Pesky?" *American Salesman,* April 1997.

Goleman, Daniel. "What Makes a Leader?" *Harvard Business Review,* November-December 1998.

Henry, Laurie J. "Persistence Leads to Accounting Performance: How to Spot a Persistent Potential Employee," *Arkansas Business and Economic Review,* Fall 1995.

Kaminsky, Marty. "Anything to Win?" *Highlights for Children,* December 1996.

Mays, Patricia J. "Gun Showers Wealth on Inventor," *The Columbus Dispatch*, April 25, 1999.

Rhoades, Brady. "The Spirit Moved Them," *The Orange County Register,* March 1, 1999.

Smith, Donna Rae. *The Power of Building Your Bright Side.* Grand Rapids, Mich.: Wynwood, 1995.

Spratling, Cassandra. "Watch Her Fly," *The Columbus Dispatch,* February 17, 1999.

Chapter 4

Applegate, Jane. "Professionals Are Chucking It All to Follow Their Passion," *The Columbus Dispatch*, April 5, 1999.

Baptist, Bob. "Hogan Gone but Hardly Forgotten," *The Columbus Dispatch*, June 2, 1999.

Canavan, Tom. "USGA Museum Unveils Ben Hogan Room," *The Columbus Dispatch*, June 9, 1999.

"D-Day Vets Agree That War Is Insane," *The Columbus Dispatch*, June 7, 1999.

Norman, Jan. "Secret of Success Sometimes a Little Something Extra," *The Orange County Register*, April 5, 1999.

Randall, Willard Sterne, and Nancy Nahra. *Forgotten Americans.* Reading, Mass.: Addison-Wesley, 1998.

Rosen, Karen. "Oh, Henry," *The Columbus Dispatch*, April 8, 1999.

"Senator Learns News about His Vietnam Injury," *The Columbus Dispatch*, March 16, 1999.

Siegel, Bernie. *Prescriptions for Living.* New York: HarperCollins, 1998.

Sinnott, Susan. *Extraordinary Asian Pacific Americans.* Chicago: Children's Press, 1993.

Strode, George. "Nicklaus Honored to Have Learned from Hogan," *The Columbus Dispatch,* June 3, 1999.

Williams, Brian. "Dallas Executive Says Boosting Employees Good for Business," *The Columbus Dispatch,* May 26, 1999.

Chapter 5

Boudreaux, Greg. "Director Competencies for the 21st Century: A Guide for New Members of the Board," *Management Quarterly*, Winter 1997.

Fletcher, Winston. "It's Make Your Mind Up Time," *Management Today,* September 1998.

Pitino, Rick. *Success Is a Choice.* New York: Broadway Books, 1997.

Satir, Virginia. *Making Contact.* Millbrae, Calif.: Celestial Arts, 1976.

Smith, Donna Rae. *The Power of Building Your Bright Side.* Grand Rapids, Mich.: Wynwood, 1995.

"Top 75: The Greatest Management Decisions Ever Made," *Management Review,* November 1998.

www.longaberger.com. November 1999.

www.manco.com. November 1999. (Manco is now a Henkel Group company.)

Chapter 6

"Buffalo Bills Linebacker Chris Spielman Takes off 1998 Season to Care for His Wife with Cancer," *Sports Illustrated,* December 14, 1998.

Lore, David. "NASA Hero Says to Shoot for the Stars," *The Columbus Dispatch,* November 19, 1998.

M.C. Hammer. interview by Nancy Snyderman. "*Good Morning America,*" ABC-TV, August 10, 1999.

McCafferty, Dennis. "All the Right Moves," *USA Weekend,* June 25-27, 1999.

Oller, Rob. "Spielman—the Father—Knows Best," *The Columbus Dispatch,* August 31, 1999.

Rabinowitz, Bill. "Spielman Hangs 'Em Up," *The Columbus Dispatch,* August 31, 1999.

Sinnot, Susan. *Extraordinary Asian Pacific Americans.* Chicago: Children's Press, 1993.

"Winning at Home," *People,* January 11, 1999.

Chapter 7

Ames, Joan Evelyn. *Mastery: Interviews with 30 Remarkable People*. Portland, Oreg.: Rudea Press, 1997.

Bachman, Justin. "Polio Shots Get Nod Over Oral Vaccine," *The Columbus Dispatch*, January 23, 2000.

Bernstein, Peter L. "How We Take Risks," *Across the Board,* February 1997.

Goleman, Daniel. "What Makes a Leader?" *Harvard Business Review,* November-December 1998.

Horowitz, Alan S. "The Sweet Smell of Failure," *Computerworld,* February 9, 1998.

Kindler, Herbert S. "The Art of Prudent Risk Taking," *Training and Development,* April 1998.

Randall, Willard Sterne, and Nancy Nahra. *Forgotten Americans: Footnote Figures Who Changed American History*. Reading, Mass.: Addison-Wesley, 1998.

Randolph, Laura B. "Dreamchasers," *Ebony*, June 1996.

Sinnott, Susan. *Extraordinary Asian Pacific Americans*. Chicago: Children's Press, 1993.

Smith, Donna Rae. *The Power of Building Your Bright Side*. Grand Rapids, Mich.: Wynwood, 1995.

Tarpley, Natasha A. "What It Takes to Start a Startup: Entrepreneurs with the Right Stuff Don't Think Much about Taking Risks or Getting Rich. Instead, They Are Obsessed with Building a Better Mousetrap," *Fortune,* June 7, 1999.

Chapter 8

Ames, Joan Evelyn. *Mastery: Interviews with 30 Remarkable People*. Portland, Oreg.: Rudea Press, 1997.

Fierman, Jaclyn. "What's Luck Got to Do with It?" *Fortune*, October 16, 1995.

Katz, Jane. "How to Get Lucky," *Cosmopolitan*, December 1997.

Kennedy, Danielle. "What Luck?" *Entrepreneur*, February 1998, p. 82.

Myers, Marc. *How to Make Luck; The Seven Secrets Lucky People Use to Succeed.* Los Angeles: Renaissance Books, 1999.

Norment, Lynn. "Roy Roberts: General Motors $100 Billion Man," *Ebony*, January 1999.

Rowe, Douglas J. "Old Man Newman: Still Winning Acclaim, Actor and Businessman Can't Help Feeling Proud," *The Columbus Dispatch*, February 21, 1999.

Shapiro, Bill. "Can You Improve Your Luck?" *Health*, January-February 1997.

Chapter 9

Bennis, Warren. "Cultivating Creative Genius," *Industry Week,* August 18, 1997.

Flynn, Gillian. "It Takes Values to Capitalize on Change," *Workforce*, April 1997.

Hays, Scott. "Exceptional Customer Service Takes the 'Ritz' Touch," *Workforce*, January 1999.

Laabs, Jennifer J. "Aristotle's Advice for Business Success," *Workforce*, October 1997.

Radice, Carol. "The Nordstrom Mystique: Customer Service That's Second to None Is the Secret of Nordstrom's Success," *Progressive Grocer,* November 1997.

Shore, Sandy. "Elway's a Success On, Off Gridiron," *The Columbus Dispatch*, January 31, 1999.

Taylor, Craig R., and Cindy Wheatley-Lovoy. "Leadership: Lessons from the Magic Kingdom," *Training and Development*, July 1998.

Chapter 10

Ashley, Herb. "The Essence of Enthusiasm," *American Salesman,* January 1997.

Blanchard, Ken, and Sheldon Bowles. "Get Gung Ho: To Create Boundless Enthusiasm, Catch Your Employees in the Act of Doing Something Right," *Success*, May 1998.

Donnelion, Sam. "Minds Set," *The Columbus Dispatch*, April 4, 1999.

Figel, Marge. "Are You Persistent or Pesty?" *American Salesman*, April 1997.

Hickey, Mary C. "The E-Factor!" *Ladies Home Journal*, September 1995.

Leigh, Pamela. "The New Spirit at Work," *Training and Development*, March 1997.

Myers, Marc. *How to Make Luck: Seven Secrets Lucky People Use to Succeed.* Los Angeles: Renaissance Books, 1999.

Chapter 11

Donnelion, Sam. "Minds Set," *The Columbus Dispatch*, April 4, 1999.

Heifetz, Ronald. "Staying Alive," *Nieman Reports*, Fall 1997.

Leider, Richard J. *The Power of Purpose—Creating Meaning in Your Life and Work.* San Francisco: Berrett-Koehler, 1997.

Leigh, Pamela. "The New Spirit at Work," *Training and Development*, March 1997.

Marton, Andrew. "Up Again When a Career Curves Down," *Association Management*, March 1999.

Perle, Ann. "What Makes Companies Well-Loved?" *Workforce*, April 1998.

Rogers, Patrick. "A Sense of Purpose," *People*, July 15, 1996.

Saari, Laura. "Pediatrician Father of Eight Dubbed Dr. Spock of the '90s," *The Orange County Register*, June 28, 1999.

Sexton, Gerry. "Invisible Assets," *Training*, June 1999.

Shepard, Alicia C. "Driving for a Goal," *USA Weekend*, August 20-22, 1999.

Sherrington, Kevin. "Armstrong: The Will, The Way," *The Dallas Morning News*, April 10, 1999.

Chapter 12

Ashabranner, Brent. *People Who Make a Difference.* New York: E. P. Dutton, 1989.

"Boss Shares His Wealth—$128 million—with His 550 Workers," *The Columbus Dispatch*, September 12, 1999.

Brokaw, Tom. *NBC Nightly News*, February 9, 1999.

Brosseau, Jim. "T&C's Guide to Volunteerism," *Town and Country*, December 1998.

Carlson, Margaret. "Once Again on the March: Colin Powell Fixed His Crusade by Working Harder and Altering His Alliances," *Time*, May 24, 1999.

Gergen, David. "The Nation's New Patriots," *U.S. News and World Report,* November 2, 1998.

"Giving Kids a Lift," *Christian Science Monitor,* September 27, 1999.

Hemphill, Thomas A. "Corporate Governance, Strategic Philanthropy, and Public Policy, *Business Horizons,* May-June 1999.

"Levy Awards Employees," *Nation's Restaurant News*, August 30, 1999.

Lewis, Diane E. "Volunteer Work Becomes Greater Emphasis of Corporate Citizenship," *The New York Times,* August 9, 1999.

Longino, Miriam. "Country Rules the Roost in Glitzy Pigeon Forge," *The Columbus Dispatch*, April 4, 1999.

Mansfield, Duncan. "Parton's Foundation Puts Books in Children's Hands," *The Columbus Dispatch*, December 27, 1998.

Mettner, Jeanne. "Giving Back," *MPLS-St. Paul Magazine,* March 1999.

Meyer, Harvey. "Helping Employees to Help Others," *Nation's Business,* March 1999.

Randolph, Laura B. "Keeping Promises," *Ebony*, July 1999.

Rowe, Douglas J. "Old Man Newman: Still Winning Acclaim, Actor and Businessman Can't Help Feeling Proud," *The Columbus Dispatch*, February 21, 1999.

Silverman, Dick. "Corporate Charity: Cause and Effect," *WWD*, August 10, 1999.

Sinnott, Susan. *Extraordinary Asian Pacific Americans*. Chicago: Children's Press, 1993.

Stossel, John. "Give Me a Break," *20/20*, ABC-TV, December 10, 1999.

Wingert, Pat. "Children's Crusade," *Newsweek*, October 4, 1999.

"Young Inventor Issues Charitable Challenge," *The Columbus Dispatch*, January 10, 1999.

Chapter 13

Cornwell, Lisa. "Educators at UC Meeting Propose Teaching Morality," *The Columbus Dispatch*, October 12, 1999.

Elkins, David N. "Spirituality," *Psychology Today*, September 1999.

Heintzman, Paul, and Glen Van Andel. "Leisure and Spirituality," *Parks and Recreation*, March 1995.

Kushner, Harold. "How Acts of Kindness Feed the Soul," *Family Circle*, November 21, 1995,

Lerner, Michael. "Spirituality in America," *Tikkun*, November-December 1998.

Lieber, Jill. "Strength Through Adversity," *USA Today*, June 2, 1999,

Remsen, Jim. "Jane Goodall Spreads a Message of Spirituality," *The Philadelphia Inquirer*, October 6, 1999.

Siegel, Bernie. *Prescriptions for Living*. New York: HarperCollins, 1998.

Smith, Deborah McCarty. "Seeking the Spirit," *University of Dayton Quarterly*, Autumn 1999.

Smith, Donna Rae. *The Power of Your Bright Side.* Grand Rapids, Mich.: Wynwood, 1995.

Swet, Peter. "Reawakening," *University of Dayton Quarterly,* Spring 1999.

"U.S. Catholic Takes a Spirituality Check," *U. S. Catholic,* October 1997.

www.gallup.org. October 11, 1999.

www.sierraclub.org. October 11, 1999.

Index

A

Act lucky, 124
Acting as if, 40-42
Actions, accountability for, 17
Attitude, adopting a lucky, 118-119

B

Beauty
  in business, 135
  in personal life, 132-133
Behavior, choosing to change
  your, 90-91
Breaks, making your own, 124-125
Business, importance of
  self-confidence in, 37-38

C

Change Your Attitude, 16, 40
Change, fear of, 77-78
Comfort zone, staying in your, 116
Companies, developing employees'
  sense of purpose, 165-169
Consciously, living, 33
Criticism vs. advice, 56-57
Cultural influences, 16
Customer service and
  self-confidence, 38-39

D

Decisions,
  accountability for, 17
  steps to making, 73
Decisive people, traits of, 72
Decisive, being, 11, 71-81
Discipline, 11, 12, , 15-30, 22-24
  and focus, 85-86
  developing personal, 19-20
  nourishing your, 21
Dreams,
  and priorities, 85-86
  following, 60-61

E

Enthusiasm, 116
  as life tool, 150

creating, 153-155
steps to developing, 151-152
Enthusiastic, being, 11, 12, 145-158
EST, 16
Excellence
in the business world, 133-136
making a personal value of, 130-133
pursuing, 130-130
Excels, 11, 129-144

F

Failure
fear of, 74-75
learning from, 108-110
"Falling forward," 109-110
Fear
and decisiveness, 74
and risks, 104
of change, 77-78
of failure, 74-75
of looking foolish, 76-77
of self, 75-76
of the unknown, 77
Focused, 11
Focused, being, 83-98

G

Goals, 13-14
adapting to reach, 17
written, 13
Goodness
in business, 135
in personal life, 131

H

Health and spirituality, 194-195

I

Identifying your values, 84-85
Improvement-oriented companies, 183-185
Improver, 11, 175-188
Insecurity, 34
Integrity, 33

J

Journaling, 12

L

Learned behavior, enthusiasm as, 147-148
Lifespring, 16
Looking foolish, fear of, 76-77
Luck,
being prepared for, 116-126
good vs. bad, 120
improving your, 123-126
Lucky, being, 11, 12, 115-128, 148

O

Opportunity costs, 20
Opportunity, seizing, 125

P

Perfection vs. reality, 87-88
Persistence, 34
  defined, 44
Persistent, being, 11, 43-53, 126
Plan of attack, devising a, 20-22, 43
Planning, 92-94
Positive, staying, 126
Priorities
  and discipline, 22
  choosing reasonable, 87
  determining your, 84
  setting, 88-89
  value-based, 84
    focusing on your, 85-94
Problems, steps to solving, 78-79
Progressive, being, 11, 55-69
Psyworld, 16
Purpose, 11, 159-174
Purposefully, living, 33

R

Responsibilities, redistributing, 19
Responsibility, taking, 17
Responsibly, living, 33
Risks
  calculated, 104-106
  taking, 100-110
Risk-taking behavior patterns, 103-104

S

Sacrifice, 89-90
Self, fear of, 75-76
Self-awareness, 72
Self-confidence, 11, 31-42
  companies that develop employees', 37-39
  developing traits that create, 32-34
  nourishing your, 32-37
Self-direction, 161-162
Self-doubt, 34
Self-esteem,
  defining, 32-33
  poor, 36-37
  traits of a healthy, 34-35
Spiritual traits, 193-194
Spiritual, being, 11, 189-199
Spirituality, 34
  benefits of, 193-195
  mixed messages about, 192-193
Steps, taking small, 91-92
Strengths and weaknesses, 20
Success, 33
  and discipline, 16
  definition of, 17
  looking like a, 34-37
  planning and preparing for, 124
  13 traits to, 11-13

T

Time, taking, 94
"Trisk," 110
Truth
  in business, 134-135
  in personal life, 131

U

Unity
  in business, 135-136
  in personal life, 133
Unknown, fear of the, 77

V

Value-based priorities, 84
  focusing on your, 85-94
Values
  identifying your, 84-85
  reviewing your, 91-92
Vision, fulfilling your, 101-102
Visionary, being, 11, 99-114
Volunteering, 176-178, 183-185

W

Work and life balance, 165-169
Workplace, excelling in the, 136-139

About the Author

Tom Bay was born and raised in southern California, where he still lives with his wife, Cathy, in Corona Del Mar. Tom's education includes a bachelor's degree in theater arts and a master's and doctorate in media communications.

Tom believes very strongly in living a balanced life, as outlined in his first book, *Change Your Attitude: Creating Success One Thought at a Time.* Tom walks his talk by balancing the work, home, community, friendship, and spiritual aspects of his life. In addition to his demanding speaking schedule, Tom enjoys family time with his wife, two sons, two grandchildren, and friends. For recreation, he runs daily and loves walking on the beach. Music is another one of his passions. Each day—often while running—Tom takes time to look within and to consult his creator about his life, his problems, his hopes, and his fears. Throughout his life, Tom has been giving back to his community in various ways; currently, he is a Make-A-Wish volunteer.

After college, Tom worked in and later owned retail stores; he also sold wholesale products on the road and worked in the finance, savings and loan, and hospitality industries. These experiences taught him much about all phases of corporate culture. Some of Tom's job titles were business owner; sales manager; savings and loan vice president, senior vice president, and executive vice president; and senior training consultant. His many work experiences have given him plenty to talk about as a motivational speaker and author.

Tom's business experience has enabled him to speak with understanding and authority to a wide variety of audiences. His topics include attitude, values, goals, accountability, responsibility, and adaptability.

As an authority on training, Tom delivers customized, industry-specific programs that target a company's individual needs by pinpointing unique programs for employees. In addition to the companies already mentioned throughout the book, Tom has worked with AT&T, the entire California State University system, Century 21, Coldwell Banker, the FBI, the Girl Scouts of America, Ingram-Micro, the National Fire Academy, Paramount Motion Pictures, Sony Corporation, the U.S. Olympic Committee, and the U.S. Postal Service.

If you enjoyed this book, you'll want to watch for Tom's book with Bernard Curtis, tentatively titled *Value Based Leadership*.